ARCHITECTURE ASIA

Journal of the Architects Regional Council Asia (ARCASIA)

I0881220

Co-Publishers

The Architectural Society of China (ASC)
9 Sanlihe Road, Beijing, China, 100835

Tongji University
1239 Siping Road, Shanghai, China, 200092

Sponsor

Tongji Architectural Design (Group) Co., Ltd.
1230 Siping Road, Shanghai, China, 200092

Contents

Editorial

This issue focuses on the development of contemporary architecture in China, curated by guest editors Zhu Xiaofeng, Thomas Chung, and Nuno Soares, appointed by the Architectural Society of China(ASC), the Hong Kong Institute of Architects(HKIA), and Architects Association of Macau(AAM). Contributions come from scholars and architects across the three institutes.

Architectural Core Elements Facing Alteration

Zhu Xiaofeng, RIBA
Guest Editor, ASC
Founding Principal, Scenic Architecture Office
Guest professor, Tongji University College of Architecture and Urban Planning

In the first quarter of the twenty-first century, the Anthropocene is undergoing significant transformations driven by environmental sustainability, social conflicts, and technological innovations. Architecture, as an extension of humanity with both cultural and technical dimensions, is no exception. Contemporary architectural practice and academia increasingly prioritize sustainability, social effect, and innovative technology. These emerging trends not only expand but also challenge the inherent elements of architecture, which has been centered around ontological concepts like site, space, tectonic and typology.

Mainland China, with its rapid construction growth over the past forty years, serves as a fertile ground where a diverse array of architectural projects is emerging. These projects consciously or unconsciously engage with the above trends, with various attitudes of embracement, resistance, or integration, yet remain a lack of systematic and comprehensive research. This editorial aims to collect a few recent samples from both practical and theoretical perspectives to foster more vitality on the study of this topic.

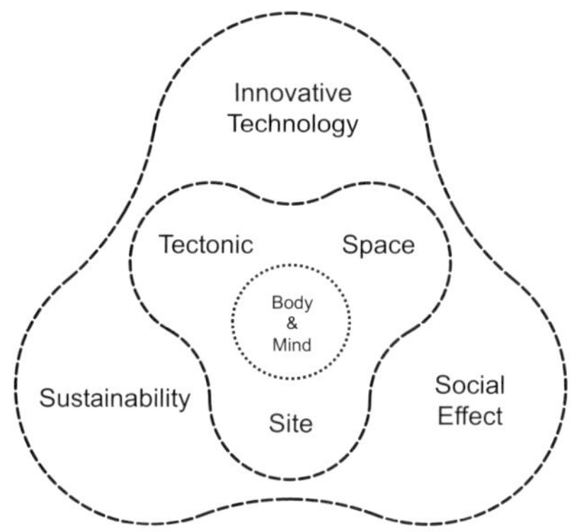

Figure 1
Architectural Core Elements Facing Alteration

The five exemplary projects include Four Studio-Houses in Ningbo by Yung Ho Chang/ Atelier FCJZ, an intrinsic pursuit of various prototypes exploring the interactions between space and human behavior; National Sliding Center for the Beijing Winter Olympics by Li Xinggang/China Architecture Design & Research Group, a dynamic structure achieving a comprehensive balance among sport, environment, technology, public engagement, and sustainable operation; Kingway Brewery Renovation in Shenzhen by Yan Meng/URBANUS, which breathes new life into an industrial legacy, transforming original structural elements and new expansions into vibrant urban spaces; RuiXue Multi-hall in Chengdu by Philip F. Yuan / College of Architecture and Urban Planning, Tongji University, a rural exhibition pavilion designed and constructed using cutting-edge intelligent robotic technology featuring a reciprocal structural system and innovative roofing materials; and Bridge of Nine Terraces in Nanjing by Zhu Xiaofeng/Scenic Architecture Office, a relaxing pedestrian bridge with a suspension structure strikingly integrated by traditional house typology and folded truss plate arch.

Additionally, two essays provide deeper theoretical insights: “The Local and the Multiplicity of Chinese Architecture” by Professor Jun-Yang Wang clarifies the fundamental concepts of local construction and advocates for a Chinese architecture grounded in local multiplicities, and “Herbalism: A Trend in Contemporary Chinese Architecture” by Professor Qing Feng utilizes the concept of Herbalism from traditional Chinese medicine theory and Martin Heidegger’s later philosophy to describe the symbiotic vision of contemporary Chinese architecture, moving beyond the simplified dialectic confrontation between modernity and tradition.

Although it is impossible to cover the full variety of architectural practices and viewpoints in contemporary mainland China, this editorial hopes that the different perspectives, wisdom, and strategies presented in these representative projects and essays will inspire a broader discussion on today’s architectural core elements facing alteration, their values, and their evolution.

Architecture and Urban Culture Beyond Territories

Thomas Chung, RIBA
Guest Editor, HKIA
Associate Professor, The Chinese University of Hong Kong

Hong Kong is renowned for its hyperdense, high-rise architecture and its unique cityscape emanating from its island-harbour-peninsula topography. Compactness, verticality and flexibility are still Hong Kong's keywords, as is the idea of the city as a "model" or laboratory for urban architectural experiments. Yet in recent years, under increasingly fierce competition in the era of globalization, Hong Kong needs to be reinventing itself. The city's self-understanding is being redefined, whereby the dialectic of tradition and innovation will drive and sustain the city's cultural creativity.

On the one hand, Hong Kong needs to preserve its distinctive characteristics such as its unrivalled international exposure, culture of openness, adaptation, and ability to embrace new ideas and integrate them into its own cultural fabric. On the other hand, Hong Kong is urged to enhance integration with the Greater Bay Area (GBA) as well as better align with national initiatives. To survive and thrive, Hong Kong must "make itself once again indispensable and irreplaceable, do what other Chinese cities cannot do, but at the same time sharing the prosperity with them"[1] (Lau, 2017).

Figure 1
T. Chung (2022) *City Beyond Territories: Multiple Hong Kongs* (越界城市: 多重香港) for "Made. Make. Making: HKSAR 25th Anniversary Exhibitions for Excellence." Roving exhibition in Hangzhou, Beijing, New York and Hong Kong to celebrate and reflect on Hong Kong's architecture culture. New York, Hong Kong: HKIA, AIA. (Exhibit panel and book cover, drawn by Lincoln Chan).

In architecture, we witness how the design of the built environment is increasingly considered as part of the city's urban culture and entering mainstream cultural discourse through major exhibitions, awards and outreach events. Since 2008, Hong Kong has been holding the Bi-City Biennale of Urbanism/Architecture (UABB) as part of the city's major cultural events every two years. The inaugural biennale, held at the former Central Police Station Compound (now Tai Kwun), was memorable for its "Refabricating City" theme that fused the city's heritage and memory, and the curation of the venue's built fabric, opening it up for the first time for public experience.

In the last two decades, pertinent topics such as sustainable design, urban renewal and heritage revitalisation, housing, harbourfront and public space have all entered public debate frequently. Likewise, continuous cultural events enabled the general public to acknowledge all these as part of creative production and cultural discourse. From the mega-scale West Kowloon Cultural District project, to the intimate scale of neighborhood projects through co-creation and place-making, multiple platforms of involving architecture as urban culture in Hong Kong have matured such that architects, built environment professionals and citizens alike are increasingly reframing their roles to broaden their involvement in envisioning the city's future.

Hong Kong's architecture stands as a testament to the region's rich history, its evolving identity, and its role within the broader context of the GBA. Compared with Macau, with its Portuguese colonial heritage, and Mainland China, with its rapid development and emphasis on large-scale infrastructure, Hong Kong's unique blend of Western and Chinese influences, its commitment to sustainability and its focus on public engagement can arguably offer valuable lessons for other cities in the GBA. Continuing this dynamic interplay of tradition, innovation, and cultural exchange, Hong Kong's ongoing reinvention through its architectural landscape will undoubtedly play a crucial role in shaping the urban culture of the region and beyond.[2]

1. Lau, L. (2017, July 6). The Return of Sovereignty of Hong Kong: Twenty Years Later. China-US Focus. https://www.chinausfocus.com/finance-economy/the-return-of-sovereignty-of-hong-kong-twenty-years-later

2. Wang, W. and Chung, T. (2010) Refabricating City: A Reflection. Hong Kong: Oxford University Press (China), 299

Macao Matters—Scarcity and Excess Reshaping Architectural Fabrication

Nuno Soares
Guest Editor, AAM
Founder and Principal Architect at UP Urban Practice
Vice-President, AAM

Macao, the densest territory in the world, is a city of contrasts where past and present converge. Its small streets coexist with large casino resorts, and its historical architectural heritage with high-rise developments. Over the last decade, two architectural projects have emerged within this context, highlighting the potential of context-specific parametric design: the Morpheus Hotel and the USJ Bamboo Pavilion. While they couldn't be more different in scale, function, tectonics, or cost, their contrasting approaches reveal how scarcity and excess can shape architectural innovation.

Designed by Zaha Hadid Architects, the Morpheus Hotel stands as a proof of concept for the articulation of parametric design with industrial fabrication. Inspired by jade carving traditions, its fluid forms, exoskeleton with metal cladding, and curved curtain glass were made possible by the industrial fabrication of non-standard building components.

The Macao gaming industry, with its high turnover and culture of spectacle, created the background for such an ambitious design and provided the investment to develop new construction technologies, and project delivery methods needed to materialise it. As a result, the overall construction industry has advanced, enabling more ambitious projects at a lower cost in the future. The Morpheus exemplifies how parametric design with industrial fabrication allows for intricate geometries to materialize precisely within industry standards. It showcases excess as a driver to push the boundaries of architectural fabrication.

In stark contrast, the USJ Bamboo Pavilion by the Department of Architecture and Design of Saint Joseph celebrates scarcity by combining humble local materials and parametric design to create an ambitious spatiality. This temporary structure is designed annually with architecture students through a community engagement process and built with traditional methods showcasing the craftsmanship of local bamboo scaffolders. Parametric design is instrumental in this project, from concept development to spatial modulation and structural definition. It expands the role of bamboo from a temporary scaffolding structure to a key material for building innovative spatial structures. The USJ Bamboo Pavilion demonstrates how academia can intersect with practice by involving students and fostering hands-on learning and innovation. It celebrates Macao's vernacular roots, bridging the gap between cultural heritage and cutting-edge fabrication, and showcasing scarcity as a viable strategy to drive contextual architectural innovation.

Both projects explore the potential of technological advancements and parametric design tools to develop architecture fabrication and create context-specific architectures. The Morpheus articulates parametric design with industrial fabrication, and the USJ Bamboo Pavilion integrates design, engagement, local materials, and craftsmanship. At the opposite edges of the spectrum, both showcase that Macao matters and that scarcity and excess remain powerful forces in shaping Macao's architectural innovation.

Figure 1 (Top) Intertwine USJ Bamboo Pavilion, by the Department of Architecture and Design at the University of Saint Joseph, 2021

Figure 2 (Bottom) Morpheus Hotel, City of Dreams by Zaha Hadid Architects, 2013-18

Beyond the Profession: Expanding the Architectural Realm to Fields of Life

SIU Kwan Yeung Marco, Member, Hong Kong Institute of Architects
LEE Chi Fung Brian, Member, Danish Association of Architects
KAN Sze Nok Sharon, Member, Hong Kong Institute of Planners
KONG Andy Padraig, Member, Hong Kong Institute of Architects
KWOK Yuen Ying Venus, Member, Hong Kong Institute of Architects

Abstract

Architecture is fast breaking free from traditional boundaries and expanding its influence, transforming cities and communities. In Hong Kong, architects and design studios are embracing new challenges and driving change by engaging with the community and addressing societal needs. They bring fresh perspectives and innovative ideas that shape our cities, communities, and society as a whole.

Architects are reshaping the built environment by designing inclusive spaces, repurposing old structures, and incorporating sustainable practices and technology. They explore diverse areas like branding, marketing, experience design, heritage interpretation, curation, new workplace patterns, and countryside development, adapting to the evolving needs of society.

Cross-disciplinary architects and design studios in Hong Kong are at the forefront of this transformation, making the built environment more inclusive, sustainable, and meaningful. Through case studies, their innovative approaches and transformative outcomes are highlighted, showcasing the potential of architects to break free from conventions and create positive change.

Author Information
SIU Kwan Yeung Marco: marcosiu.kwanyeung@gmail.com
LEE Chi Fung Brian: brianlcf@gmail.com
KAN Sze Nok Sharon: snsharonkan@gmail.com
KONG Andy Padraig: padraigkong@gmail.com
KWOK Yuen Ying Venus: vyyk428@gmail.com

Keywords

Participatory, marketing, experience, activity, curation, policy-making

Figure 1
Five Tallest Buildings in Hong Kong, ink painting (Wilson Shieh, 2011)

Figure 2
Public engagement for public housing well-being through design-thinking and participatory design by Housing Bureau (HKSARG, 2023)

1. Introduction: From Project Delivery to Beyond Traditional Boundaries

Architecture has long been associated with the design and construction of buildings, shaping the physical environment in which we live, work, and play. However, the role of architects is no longer confined to traditional boundaries. As society evolves, architects are also embracing new challenges and expanding their realm to areas that extend far beyond the conventional scope of the profession. This shift has the potential to reshape our cities, communities, and even our way of life. Architects have traditionally focused on project delivery, ensuring that buildings are designed and constructed according to the client's requirements. However, they are now venturing beyond these confines, seeking to engage with the broader community to address societal needs. Architects are becoming catalysts for change, initiating projects that have a lasting impact on the social, cultural, and economic fabric of a place. In the recent years, architects in Hong Kong have been pushing the boundaries and expanding their influence into various fields of practice, with small-scaled but creative commissions. Due to their reduced scale, these projects often explore and incorporate new ideas from emergent discourses such as sustainability, modular construction and participatory design.

This essay explores the impact of architects entering cross-disciplinary territories and examines how young design studios are redefining what it means to be an architect and transforming the built environment, bringing in fresh perspectives and bold ideas. They are not bound by tradition, but driven by a passion to make a difference. These studios and architects embody experimentation, adaptability, and interdisciplinary collaboration, allowing them to explore new avenues and extend their reach beyond conventional architectural practice.

They approach the reimagination of housing design by public engagements with the reinvention of public open spaces to foster community well-being. They are involved in the design of transitional housing, paying deep attention to the communal space, so as to encourage residents to making new connections and nurture social empowerment. These studios are also reshaping the residential clubhouses by delivering landmark design features for branding and marketing to create value. They create engaging spaces that go beyond transactions, transforming retail environments into dynamic and inspiring places. In the civic and public realms, architects and design studios are reimagining public open spaces and parks with architectural interventions in the form of pavilions, installations, and urban furniture. They aim to create vibrant, inclusive, and sustainable environments that foster social interaction, cultural exchange, and a sense of community ownership with identity and purpose. Revitalizing heritage sites and curating artifacts is another area in which architects are expanding their influence, combining design expertise with historical preservation principles to breathe new life into old structures while respecting their cultural significance, as well as curate historic artifacts on how visitors shall interpret the heritage. Architects are also working with urban planners, engineers, policymakers, and communities to envision sustainable and livable cities, and on the careful engagement with the existing cultural context and ecology habitat, especially in a shifting paradigm of workplaces.

Architects that are going into cross-disciplinary zones, as well as the emergence of design studios in Hong Kong are redefining the possibilities of architecture. They are expanding their influence beyond traditional boundaries and making a positive impact on various aspects of human existence. From housing and commercial spaces to civic environments, heritage preservation, and urban planning, architects are shaping a more inclusive, sustainable, and meaningful built environment. This essay will delve into specific case studies, highlighting the innovative approaches and transformative outcomes achieved by architects who venture beyond traditional boundaries.

2. Housing and Residential Developments

2.1 Design for Communal: Beyond Typological Evolution and into Participatory Design

Architects are breaking traditional boundaries in public housing projects in Hong Kong. They are addressing the many issues within public spaces and also communal well-being, going beyond the typical compact unit design. Design studios are also participating in government-dominated pilot projects for transitional housing. Architects prioritize creating inclusive environments that promote social interaction and a sense of belonging. They engage with local communities, involving them in the design process, and co-create spaces that reflect their needs. This approach improves the built environment's quality, strengthens community bonds, and fosters social cohesion.

Public housing in Hong Kong has evolved rapidly from its first prototypical "resettlement estates" in 1963 to a steady typological evolution and optimization of the public housing typology, in terms of efficiency, density and buildability. The Housing Bureau initiated the "Well-Being" project in late 2022 to study how existing communal spaces in as-built estates could be improved through participatory design processes led by the design studio Architecture Commons, to develop a Well-being Design Guide.[1] This was the first large-scale public engagement project focused on the well-being of public housing, where data and public opinion were collected through qualitative research and interviews with residents. These will presumably be reflected in the implementation stage when the Bureau liaises with local practices—meaning more opportunities for young offices in this new front. The emerging discourse on sustainability also gave opportunities to young architects to contribute to the design of communal public open spaces via different channels. Modular Integrated Construction (MiC), emerged on the Hong Kong construction scene in late 2017 and constructed "transitional housing" projects and held its first competition in 2022 titled SDG Eco-Village, with a focus on the juxtaposition of building blocks and the communal spaces in between them. Common-Ground architects, a young local firm won this competition and will become lead consultants for MiC's construction in Kam Tin.[2] The scheme is titled STEPS—as in, a stepping-stone—on the belief that the essence of a transitional housing is not merely to provide a residence, but to also function as a stepping-stone for residents to become empowered.[3] The competition's jury was of the view that the architectural design quality of the construction was high and would help give the project an attractive image. The SDG eco features are well integrated, and not just thrown in as add-ons, and there is real consideration to both social and environmental sustainability issues. The central boulevard provided spaces for community gathering, healthy exercise, and many multi-people activities. The roof terraces provide spaces for chats and

Figure 3
STEPS was awarded the first prize in the Architectural Design Idea Competition for SDG Eco-Village's transitional housing (Common Ground Design, 2011)

Figure 4
A green lung urban framing in the common garden and clubhouse of Pavilia Farm emphasizes "urban pastoral living" (Snøhetta, 2022)

community gatherings and enables the creation of a lively village. The design of the centralized farm with inspiring activities is interesting and worth further exploration. The housing blocks, too, look interesting, featuring a common balcony at the end of the corridors and an overall well thought out distribution of common facilities.

2.2 Design for Branding: Clubhouse as Design Typology in Private Residential Developments

Architecture is increasingly being leveraged as a tool for branding and identity creation. Private residential projects of the last few decades focused more on maximizing views, minimizing auxiliary spaces, and mapping the most efficient floor plan to maximize developer profits. Architects are now collaborating with developers and marketers to design buildings that go beyond their functional purpose. The rising popularity of exclusive spaces, such as the clubhouse concept, has demonstrated how architecture can be used to create unique and immersive experiences that resonate with specific target audiences. These spaces serve as powerful branding tools, attracting individuals who seek to be part of a selective lifestyle or community.

Completed in 2022, the residential complex Pavilia Farm in Tai Wai, at first glance follows the familiar typology of the transportation cum topside residential complex that is commonly seen in Hong Kong, with residential towers situated on top of a shopping mall and podium garden. The key difference in Pavilia Farm is its emphasis on the design of its common facilities that serve its residents. The developer enlisted international "starchitect" company, Snøhetta, as the lead designer of the generous 2,800-square-meter area, in collaboration with other smaller local and foreign firms, such as Ohtori, Avanto, and Daydreamers, integrating Nordic, Japanese, and local creative design aspects and functions for an urban pastoral living.[4] International fads such as organic food and farm-to-table concepts have been employed in the longhous the Farm Pavilion, which faces a terraced landscape that doubles as a miniature farm; the Tea House features a waterfall spectacle and references an oriental Zen theme that is commonly seen in hotel projects. This not only reflects the changing taste of the Hong Kong middle class but also a shift of focus for developers, from unit layouts to marketing and promoting architectural designs based on communal facilities and activities. This new trend of "feature clubhouses" has opened up design opportunities for emergent international and local firms to design small pavilions, interiors, and feature landscapes. This benefits the developer and architects reciprocally, as designs become branding tools for developers, and also advertisement for the design firms themselves.

3. Retail Spaces

3.1 Design for Marketing: Repurposing Old Clusters as Asset Enhancement

In response to the growing need for sustainable development, architects are now exploring innovative strategies for repurposing existing structures. By breathing new life into old clusters, architects can enhance their value and contribute to the revitalization of the urban areas the buildings are situated in. This approach not only minimizes the environmental impact, but also preserves the cultural heritage of a place while meeting the demands of modern living.

Figure 5
T.O.P (This is Our Place) transformed a 1980s former government complex into a modern office and retail-entertainment hub (Aedas, 2018)

Figure 6
The Oculus at K11 MUSEA atrium; the studio was involved in interior design and digital crafting (LAAB, 2021)

Due to the shortage of vacant land for major urban developments, many developers are now focusing their sights on older generation malls as candidates for redevelopment. These projects are usually in prime sites to be refurbished and rebranded, for which architects are not only commissioned to upgrade existing infrastructure to facilitate functionality and the latest sustainability standards, but also to engage in marketing and asset enhancement.

In the community malls category, LINK shopping malls are pioneers in upgrading outdated and worn-out open-air estate malls to serve their adjacent public housing cluster. A remarkable example is the Lok Fu Plaza, where a new outdoor plaza, enclosed by a steel truss roof, provides an apt venue for many community events. In the high-end retail tier, the original Pacific Place mall underwent a design overhaul in 2011 spearheaded by the international firm Studio Heatherwick. The existing terraces were transformed into enclosed gardens, alfresco dining spots, and places for socializing. For the young demographic, the recently completed T.O.P. mall, designed by Aedas,[5] revamps a worn-out government building by puncturing a new atrium through its existing structure, its raw industrial aesthetics capitalizing on the as-found culture popular amongst young people.

3.2 Design for Experience: Landmark as a Collection of Design Features

Architects are now designing landmarks that transcend mere aesthetics to become immersive experiences. These landmarks are conceived as a collection of design features that engage all the senses, leaving a lasting impression on visitors.

As developers and architects are becoming more brand-conscious and social-media-conscious, new malls are now punctuated by smaller pockets of space with various spot attractions and features, rather than highlight holistic designs. These are often small-scale bespoke designs and embody the contemporary retail experience as "Instagram-friendly" attractions, ushering in a new paradigm of experience placemaking.

Victoria Dockside is a radical example of such transformation via a collection of feature designs. It is a commercial development abutting a landmark site, lining a section of the Victoria Harbour and connects directly to the Avenue of Stars, a prominent tourist attraction. In a typical mall project, a single firm or office usually leads the design with the help of an executive architect. Victoria Dockside has employed a multifaceted approach: 1. doubling its function as a mall-cum-museum, displaying an extensive collection of artworks and furniture in its common arcade; and 2. featuring an amalgamation of small-scale art pieces, spaces, and pavilions within the same mall. These features are co-designed by a plethora of offices, including local firms LAAB architects and AB Concept, and international ones such as OMA and James Corner Field Operations,[6] with each office tasked with designing a parcel within the complex, which results in an assemblage of designs within one complex. As malls become more Instagrammable, this not only benefits developers by extending free exposure and advertising through social media, but also gives architects more unique commissions and design opportunities for young offices.

Figure 7
Placemaking installations at North Point East Coast Park (ARTA Architects, 2023)

Figure 8
Water Capsule Submarine Pavilion at Tamar Promenade (New Office Works, 2023)

4. Public Space

4.1 Design for Activity: Intervention from Pavilion to Furniture at Harbourfront

Architecture is no longer limited to the construction of large-scale buildings. Architects are intervening at various scales, from pavilions and installations to furniture design. By reimagining public spaces and designing adaptable structures, architects are enhancing the vibrancy and functionality of urban areas. The revitalization of Harbourfront, for example, creates flexible spaces that can accommodate a range of activities, from outdoor performances and markets to leisure and relaxation. Presently, a series of innovative placemaking strategies are reshaping the waterfronts of Hong Kong Island, emphasizing inclusivity and public involvement. Previously disjointed public spaces along the harborfront, spanning from the eastern edge in Shau Kei Wan, along the commercial node in Central to the western terminus in Kennedy Town, have been synergized and linked up by a series of "Points of Interest." The "Harbourfront Shared Space"[7] explores diverse design prepositions and management models. This project typology has empowered local emerging architects and designers to design vibrant installations and furniture, with an aim to foster active engagement, creative endeavors, as well as respond to the context of harbor.

The K-farm project, designed by Avoid Obvious Architects[8] at the Belcher's Bay Promenade, proposed a transformation from its previous role as a public cargo working area by planning and integrating various building elements. Notably, the indoor aqua farm has provided a unique opportunity to explore functional community farming and aquaculture in a compact setting and offers new experiences for the public. Another example can be found with North Point East Coast Park, where ARTA Architects[9] created and energized the area through the incorporation of unique sculptures and art installations, optimizing the family-friendly pathway with Instagram-worthy pop-ups and follies.

The Art@Harbor event at Tamar Park and the Central and Western District Promenade (Central Section) displayed nine sets of interactive art installations and three 3-D floor graphics.[10] It was a collaborative effort between local young architects, artists, and art-tech partners, showcasing a seamless blend of creativity and technology. One of the urban furniture featured, the Ornithopter—a creation by HIR Studio[11]—successfully engages with visitors by providing a tactile experience. Inspired by Leonardo da Vinci's ornithopter sketches and the historical 1911 bi-plane test flight in Hong Kong, the Ornithopter is equipped with a pair of double-stack flapping wings which can be manually operated by a bicycle mechanical system. Another intervention, the Water Capsule Submarine Pavilion, a creation by New Office Works,[12] offers a captivating exploration of the interplay between land and water, and day and night. Within this droplet-shaped structure, a dual-layered inflatable skin and tunnel structure offer both transparency and picturesque views to the harbor, and an experience of the water-undulating phenomena.

Architects formulate a pioneering approach to invite the community toward waterfronts with the use of pavilions, installations, and furniture. These examples exemplify and promote a high degree of flexibility and inclusiveness by introducing interventions and creating activities at open spaces along the harborfront. The initiative provides young designers and architects with opportunities to actively contribute to placemaking for communal activities along the harborfront.

5. Heritage

5.1 Design for Heritage Interpretation: Adaptive Reuse and the Mix of Old and New

Preserving cultural heritage while adapting to modern needs is a delicate balance that architects strive to achieve. Adaptive reuse is gaining prominence as a sustainable approach to revitalizing historic buildings. By blending old and new elements, architects create a dialog between the past and the present, allowing heritage to be experienced in a contemporary context. This approach not only conserves architectural heritage but also enriches the urban fabric by creating dynamic spaces that celebrate history and culture.

Architects encounter significant challenges when transforming historic structures into public spaces. By considering a heritage lifecycle, public requirements, and political agenda, the objective is to repurpose, rejuvenate, and reintroduce these spaces to the community. Through comprehensive research and study of history, architects work to preserve both tangible and intangible aspects. In Hong Kong, heritage extension has been a successful approach to adaptive reuse, bridging the past with the future through the introduction of innovative interventions that maximize the development potential.

PMQ transformed from its origins as the Former Police Married Quarters in Sheung Wan[13] to become a renowned landmark for creative industries. Designated as an iconic "Grade 3" historical building by the Antiquities and Monuments Office, the repurposing demanded careful and sensitive preservation efforts. Embracing the core principle of revitalization,[14] architects blended modern functionality with the conservation of the archaeological relics or heritage elements to offer new extensions to create inviting indoor venues.

The University of Chicago Campus in Hong Kong, designed by Revery Architecture[15] (formerly Bing Thom Architects), is situated on a heritage-protected site that housed a military facility and a detention center. The innovative design approach in this project suspends the new extension above the historic remnants and verdant trees, minimizing any disturbance to the ecological landscape. The architects' goal here is to honor both the existing heritage buildings and the natural environment, including the surrounding public hiking trails.

5.2 Design for Curation: Multimedia Integration of Archaeological Narration

Architects are embracing multimedia integration to curate narratives and enhance the visitor experience in archaeological sites. Through the use of technology, such as augmented reality and interactive displays, architects bring history to life, transforming passive observers into active participants. By creating immersive environments that combine storytelling with architectural design, architects enable visitors to engage with the past in a meaningful and educational way.

Apart from the adaptive reuse of heritage buildings, there are also other ongoing archaeological projects in Hong Kong. The Lung Tsun Stone Bridge located at Kai Tak was previously buried but was discovered during archaeological excavations in 2008. Given its historical significance, the government proposed to establish a conservation corridor to preserve the Lung Tsun Stone Bridge remnant in-situ.

Figure 9
New extension of PMQ (Thomas Chau Architects, 2014)

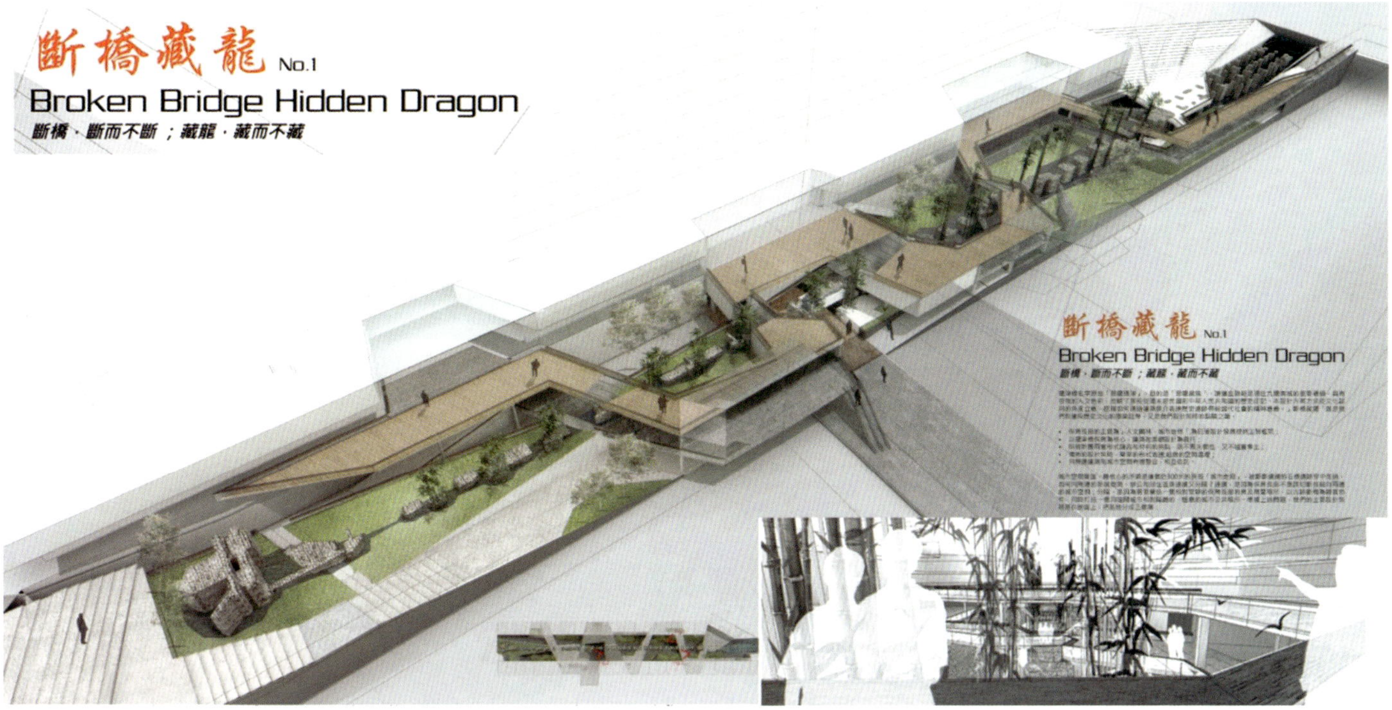

Figure 10
Winning scheme of Lung Tsun Stone Bridge design competition (Development Bureau, HKSARG, 2014)

The role of the design and executive architect of this Preservation Corridor is assigned to the Architectural Services Department,[16] handling the project as an in-house project. Through an open design competition, the first schematic design was selected from the winning entry.[17] This project employs a heritage interpretation strategy with carefully designed viewing angles that communicate with audiences. The architect also acted as a curator by selecting and implementing expositions of multimedia technologies to provide innovative experiences to the visitors on-site and at the exhibitions. This heritage project will become the centerpiece of the Kai Tak redevelopment zone and will also become the largest outdoor historical museum in Hong Kong.

6. New Development Areas

6.1 Design for Worklife: Reimagining Urban Morphology

The changing nature of work and the rise of remote and flexible working arrangements have prompted architects to reimagine urban morphology. Architects play a vital role in designing innovative workspaces that cater to the evolving needs of the workforce—agile workspaces that facilitate co-working and optimize underutilized office areas resulting from flexible work arrangements through the design of adaptable floor plans, modular office configurations, and shared work areas capable of accommodating diverse work styles, to foster creativity, collaboration, and productivity.

In the traditional development model, architects were typically assigned a land parcel and they worked independently, often without sufficient consideration for neighboring land use and compatibility with the surrounding environment. However, the establishment of the central business district (CBD) on Kau Yi Chau Artificial Islands presents architects with a unique opportunity to reassess their role as placemakers, through the effective utilization of architecture.

The artificial islands offer a blank canvas for holistic planning, enabling architects to strategically position developments within the area. This presents an opportunity to create a new identity for the central business district by ensuring a cohesive and compatible building profile throughout the CBD. The heterogeneous land use provision in a CBD—by integrating public spaces and social services—offers places of respite relaxation and opportunity for social interaction amidst the bustling commercial environment. While CBD3 would be located in the heart of the island tip,[18] increasing its porosity toward the waterfront will be an important strategy to ensure the provision of a diverse urban experience.

6.2 Design for Countryside: Policy Influence on Adaptive Reuse and Conservation Ecology

Architects are increasingly involved in shaping policies that govern sustainable development in rural areas. By advocating for adaptive reuse and conservation ecology, architects contribute to the preservation of natural landscapes and cultural heritage. They work closely with policymakers to develop guidelines that promote responsible land use and ensure the long-term sustainability of rural communities. Through innovative design strategies, architects are revitalizing countryside areas, repurposing existing structures, and integrating sustainable practices that harmonize with the surrounding environment.

In the Northern Metropolis, characterized by brownfields and areas of cultural heritage and ecological significance,

Figure 11
Artist impression of the Kau Yi Chau Artificial Islands (Development Bureau, 2022)

Figure 12
San Tin Technopole (Civil Engineering and Development Department and Planning Department, 2023)

architects are entrusted with a crucial role in the transformation of idle structures, wetlands, and other natural resources. This responsibility entails seamlessly integrating these elements with new developments, including technopoles, residential areas, and commercial developments.[19] By skillfully knitting the existing context with the envisioned developments, architects contribute to the preservation of cultural heritage, the enhancement of ecological sustainability, and the overall harmonious transformation from the subjects' current composition to a new envisioned use, while strengthening new focal points for cultural exchange, education, and community engagement.

One notable example is the vacated barracks from World War II and a historic Hindu Temple that neighbors the Queen's Hill housing development in Fanling. The adaptive reuse of the remaining barracks becomes a matter of vital importance through their repurposing into the community space, for instance, community kitchens where residents can come together to share meals and foster a sense of camaraderie and cultural exchange. Additionally, the spacious barracks could serve as venues for screening events and showcasing movies or documentaries that celebrate the diverse heritage and stories of the local community.

7. Conclusion

Architecture, once confined to the realm of designing structures, has transcended its traditional boundaries and embarked on a journey of exploration and transformation. Architects and design studios in Hong Kong are at the forefront of this movement, venturing into diverse fields of practice and tiers of life, reshaping the way we perceive and interact with our surroundings. By embracing participatory design, branding, marketing, experience design, heritage interpretation, curation, work-life balance, and countryside development, architects are demonstrating their ability to adapt and evolve, to address the changing needs and aspirations of society. The expansion of architecture beyond its traditional boundaries presents a wider realm of possibility and speculation. It has already shown its transformative impact on various aspects of life, prompting us to imagine a future where architects go beyond their conventional limits.

What if architects not only created physical spaces but also drove social change? What if their influence extended to addressing global challenges like climate change, inequality, and urbanization? In this future, architects would lead the creation of resilient communities, collaborating with experts from different fields to tackle complex issues; they would shape a global agenda that integrates sustainability, equity, and cultural preservation. Imagine architects playing a vital role in developing smart cities that blend technology, data, and human-centric design. These cities would adapt to the needs of their inhabitants, optimizing energy, transportation, and resources using AI, virtual reality, and data analytics. Architects would design spaces that enhance well-being, foster creativity, and cultivate a harmonious relationship between humans and their surroundings. In this future, architects would also become custodians of memory and cultural heritage; they would weave narratives of history and tradition into contemporary designs, preserving not only physical structures but also intangible cultural practices and identities. Architects would bridge generational gaps, forging a collective memory rooted in history and open to innovation.

However, this expansion into diverse fields poses challenges. Architects must navigate complex ethical, cultural, and social landscapes, understanding the intricate interplay between design, power dynamics, and human experience. Inclusivity, equity, and amplifying marginalized voices are crucial commitments. While the future of architecture remains uncertain, the potential for architects to shape the world is vast. The emergence of young design studios reminds us of the creative forces within the profession. By embracing experimentation, collaboration, and purpose, architects can create a future that is architecturally stunning, socially just, environmentally sustainable, and culturally rich.

The emergence of architects venturing beyond the confines of their profession in Hong Kong serves as a testament to the limitless potential of architecture as a transformative force. Through case studies and real-world examples, the impact of participatory design, branding, marketing, experience design, heritage interpretation, curation, work-life balance, and countryside development can be observed. Architects are breaking free from the constraints of convention, leveraging their skills and creativity to create positive change that extends far beyond the physical realm. As architects expand their realm into these diverse tiers of life, they are not only reshaping the built environment but also redefining their role in society. Thus, they have become catalysts for change, actively engaging with communities, addressing societal needs, and bringing fresh perspectives and innovative ideas to the table. Architects are no longer confined to their traditional profession; they have become advocates, storytellers, and problem solvers.

Let us imagine a future where architects transcend their conventional roles and become catalysts for a harmonious and resilient existence. Embracing the speculative nature of this journey, we can explore possibilities beyond traditional boundaries. By doing so, we redefine the essence of architecture and its potential to shape our collective destiny.

Notes

1. " 'Well.Being' Public Housing Well-being Journey," Well.Being, Housing Bureau, Hong Kong Housing Authority, HKSARG, accessed October 31, 2023, https://housingwellbeing.hk/en.
2. "Results Announcement: Architectural Design Idea Competition for SDG Eco-Village Transitional Housing," Professional Green Building Council, 2019, https://www.hkpgbc.org/event_details.php?id=1&fbclid=IwAR2_Tr3W8-g9ZraLtmhS5DXdmGcZtWkeN2XGcDLqdmNoyJENKYKBNCnrelU.
3. "SDG Eco-Village Transitional Housing," Common Ground Design, 2019, https://www.common-ground.hk/uncategorized/sdg-eco-village-transitional-housing.
4. "Pavilia Farm," *Construction Plus Asia*, 2019, https://www.constructionplusasia.com/hk/pavilia-farm.
5. "T.O.P This is Our Place," Aedas, 2019, https://www.aedas.com/en/what-we-do/architecture/retail/t-o-p-this-is-our-place.
6. "Victoria Dockside Launches Hong Kong to a New Cultural Frontier – Adrian Cheng Creates First Wave of Excitement at the 3m Sqft Art and Design District," New World Development Company Limited, 2018, https://www.nwd.com.hk/content/victoria-dockside-launches-hong-kong-new-cultural-frontier-adrian-cheng-creates-first-wave-2.
7. "Harbourfront Shared Space," Harbourfront Commission, 2023, HKSARG, https://www.hfc.org.hk/en/hss/index.html.
8. "K-farm: Smart Urban Farming," Avoid Obvious Architects, accessed November 1, 2023, https://aoarchitect.us/projects/k-farm-smart-urban-farming.
9. "The Harbour Wave 流動維港," ARTA Architects, accessed November 1, 2023, https://arta.archi/project/the-harbour-wave-%E6%B5%81%E5%8B%95%E7%B6%AD%E6%B8%AF.
10. "Art@Harbour," Leisure and Cultural Services Department, Museums, 2022, HKSARG, https://www.museums.gov.hk/en/web/portal/artatharbour.html#aah-projects.
11. "The Ornithopter 夢想實驗號," HIR Studio Limited, 2019, https://www.hir-studio.com/projects/the-ornithopter-%E5%A4%A2%E6%83%B3%E5%AF%A6%E9%A9%97%E8%99%9F-%E3%80%80.
12. "NOW 76 | Water Capsule Submarine," New Office Works, accessed November 1, 2023, https://www.newofficeworks.com/project/now-76-water-capsule-submarine.
13. "Project," Thomas Chow Architects, 2019, http://www.thomaschow.com.hk/project.
14. "Introduction and Background," Conserve and Revitalise Hong Kong Heritage, Commissioner for Heritage's Office, HKSARG, accessed November 1, 2023, https://www.heritage.gov.hk/en/heritage-conservation-policy-historic-buildings/former-police-married-quarters-on-hollywood-road/introduction-background/index.html.
15. "University of Chicago's Hong Kong Campus," Revery Architecture, accessed November 1, 2023, https://reveryarchitecture.com/projects/university-of-chicago-hong-kong-campus.
16. "Lung Tsun Stone Bridge Preservation Corridor at Kai Tak–龍津石橋保育長廊," Harbourfront Commission, 2017, Architectural Services Department, HKSARG, https://www.hfc.org.hk/filemanager/files/TFKT_20171101_ppt_item3.pdf.
17. "Blog Articles from Former Secretary... (56)," Development Bureau, 2014, HKSARG, https://www.devb.gov.hk/en/home/Blog_Archives1/index_id_56.html.
18. "Preliminary Proposal – Broad Land Use," Kau Yi Chau Artificial Islands, Development Bureau, HKSARG, accessed November 1, 2023, https://www.centralwaters.hk/en/broad-land-use.
19. "Home," Northern Metropolis | San Tin Technopole, Civil Engineering and Development Department and Planning Department, HKSARG, accessed November 1, 2023, https://nm-santintech.hk/en.

Figure Credits

Figure 1: Five Tallest Buildings in Hong Kong, 2011 (Courtesy of Wilson Shieh)
Figure 2: Public engagement for public housing well-being through design-thinking and participatory design, 2023 (Courtesy of Housing Bureau, HKSARG)
Figure 3: STEPS by Common Ground Design, winner of the first prize in the Architectural Design Idea Competition for SDG Eco-Village transitional housing, 2011 (Courtesy of Common Ground Design)
Figure 4: A green lung urban framing in the common garden and clubhouse of Pavilia Farm emphasizing "urban pastoral living," 2022 (Courtesy of Snøhetta)
Figure 5: T.O.P (This is Our Place) transforming a 1980s former government complex into a modern office and retail-entertainment hub, 2018 (Courtesy of Aedas)
Figure 6: The Oculus at K11 MUSEA Atrium, involving interior design and digital crafting, 2021 (Courtesy of LAAB)
Figure 7: Placemaking installations at North Point East Coast Park, 2023 (Courtesy of ARTA Architects)
Figure 8: Water Capsule Submarine Pavilion at Tamar Promenade, 2023 (Courtesy of New Office Works)
Figure 9: New extension of PMQ, 2014 (Courtesy of Thomas Chau Architects)
Figure 10: Winning scheme of Lung Tsun Stone Bridge design competition organized, 2014 (Courtesy of the Development Bureau, HKSARG)
Figure 11: Artist impression of the Kau Yi Chau Artificial Islands, 2022 (Courtesy of the Development Bureau, HKSARG)
Figure 12: San Tin Technopole, 2023 (Courtesy of the Civil Engineering and Development Department and Planning Department)

An Evolving Human Landscape in the Pearl River Delta

Wallace CHANG, FHKIA, RIBA, AIA (Assoc.)

Abstract

When the Great Bay Area was first announced and articulated as an economic engine, the Pearl River Delta in southern Guangdong Province, where capitals, production, and innovations were concentrated, was overlooked. Besides the political empowerment, why and how the cluster cities collaborating toward a new destination should, however, be understood as a holistic landscape with a humanistic perspective. If the connections through the flow of "waters within the blue territories" in history might provide a clue to recent developments of the region, the investigation of its traditional and evolving cultures is suggesting an avant-garde spirit long embedded since its inception of an alternative territory. When local realities riding on pragmatism over the cultivated human landscape are treasured over any imposition of ideology, the resultant urban and architectural expressions may portray a new mindscape of the people in the future.

Keywords

Pearl River Delta, flow-of-lives, human landscape, evolving identity, cultural manufacturing

Author Information
Wallace CHANG: phchang001@gmail.com

Figure 1
PRD Vs GBA in 1979 & 2019

1. Divided Coherence

Perhaps the proximity of the '9+2'[1] cluster cities, now known as the Great Bay Area (GBA)[2] is enabling an energized performance to make the region a powerhouse of emerging economy in the next century. When Huawei in Dongguan is efficiently making a new smart phone, Shenzhen's IT engineers are engaged to upgrade corresponding virtual environment, and while Hong Kong is launching its fin-tech infrastructure, Macau is applying it in the entertainment industries. So, is it because cross-border highways and high-speed train networks developed in the last two decades that are overriding the separating waterways and connecting these cities together, or is something else in place? When this seamlessly synchronized synergy is spontaneously responding to new ideas from minds-alike, then the question is "what makes the minds of people from the Pearl River Delta (PRD) cities 'think and act together'?" (Figure 1).

The coherence of these cities is not a coincidence but started from the coastal defense ports' alliance when Portuguese travelers were first embarking at Macau five centuries ago and later British traders at Hong Kong. To receive 'foreigners,' these coastal ports acting as front gates to the Empire were providing a buffer to protect the provincial capital of Guangzhou. With their strategic positioning of open ports safeguarded with a chain of coastal fortresses, like Dapeng and Tungchung, along the coastlines of the Pearl River Delta, they were supporting the daily supplies for the fleets and at the same time protecting the region's territorial integrity.

This framing of territorial disposition had offered an intrinsic cultural understanding of the region as an outward-looking region with multi-level considerations. The formation of the territorial vertices of Guangzhou, Hong Kong, and Macau was aligned to a specific "delta" within which the waterscape began to connect these land/water geographical nodes into a meaningful entity. Among them, there were a multitude of water-borne communities, like the Daan people who resided in the half-land-half-water bays of Lai Chi Wan (Guangzhou), Aberdeen (Hong Kong), and Fai Chi Kei (Macau), to provide alternative networks of transportation, food and water, and even culture in the PRD (Figure 2). These frequent communications between water-borne communities with the European newcomers had interlaced with land-borne communities through a common means of water transports. Shuttling among water bodies including the PRD's fishing grounds, harbors, shores, and webs of waterways penetrating inland, these water-borne people were connecting European traders to make business as well as to bring along a reverse perspective, new ideas from the oceans instead of taking orders from the continents. This cultural shift of welcoming new ideas from the world beyond had enabled this region to "think otherwise" with an open attitude toward "newness" that cultivated the people of the PRD to be receptive to any cultural changes and develop pragmatic mindsets.

2. Mutated Adaptation

In the early Colonial Period, urban developments of Guangzhou, Hong Kong, and Macau, such as arcaded shop-houses and urban public spaces like "prayas" in Macau and "squares" in Hong Kong, were reflections of this pragmatic attitude to integrating imported urban cultures into local conditions. These cultural mutations in architectural forms and urban spaces when transplanted locally had been shaping both daily life and perceived

Figure 2
Water-borne communities along the Pearl River Delta

images of these cities. Thus, an old saying "Guangzhou City, Hong Kong Praya, Macau Street" described vividly the urban impressions of this tri-city relationship in terms of their respective presence and urban scale (Figure 3).

Although there were similarities in the arcade streets in the three cities to address the local climate and shopping behaviour, they varied subtly in terms of scale, style, and construction skill. For example, Shangxiajiu in Guangzhou was connected with higher headroom arcades, and the arcaded street of Nathan Road in Hong Kong was aligned with banyan trees, whereas smaller-scale arcades along Avenida de Almeida Ribeiro in Macau were formed by Mediterranean-style building blocks.

Conceived as an inseparable region to protect the provincial capital (Guangzhou) with two extended arms of outer towns (Hong Kong and Macau), the cultural inter-flows were bilateral instead of triangular where the dominant local culture, Cantonese, was hosting two guest European "subcultures," English and Portuguese, from two ends of the colonial cities respectively.

Beyond the built environment, other cultural evidence was the Cantonese opera, *Red Boat*, named after boats carrying performers shuttled between performance venues among the three cities in the PRD. Besides the Cantonese opera having continuously absorbed influences from opera elements of other Chinese regions, the musical instruments included those in Western operas, like violins, trumpets, and so on. The Cantonese opera being an inclusive art form to entertain the elite class as well as to educate the general public, the performances took place seasonally and reached communities in both urban and rural areas (Figure 4). Due to their nomadic nature, performance troops brought the latest cultural trends, sometimes revolutionary thinking, from the "outer towns" of Hong Kong, and Macau to the "inner city" of Guangzhou. These inter-city cultural flows enabled Cantonese-speaking communities among different political regimes to share a common interest in the external world.

3. Independent Growth

After World War II and civil wars in China, then the "closed-door policy," the hierarchy of capital-township among Guangzhou, Hong Kong, and Macau was dissolved. For over three decades, Guangzhou had been drifting among political struggles while both Hong Kong and Macau were absorbing Western cultures as any other cities in the world. Acting as 'valves' to buffer filtered cultural impacts as well as 'windows' to view the outside world beyond the "closed door," both cities were developed independently with strong Western cultural influences.

Without any political overlays, Hong Kong and Macau were riding on the post-war movements of rebuilding the city and equivalent "million-home" housing program as their European hosts. In 1946, there was a critical planning exercise for the city of Hong Kong when Patrick Abercrombie, the master British planner for London, was invited to propose the first comprehensive framework of modern urban planning. The first urban planning had structured the city with grids (100m x 40-45m) for mixed use urban blocks intermixing zones for light industries along with residential districts. The 'Abercrombie Plan' had demarcated the overall direction of Hong Kong toward a 'light industrial' city where living and working were basically intermixed within the urban districts. In fact, the physical configuration of these urban ensembles had induced an urban culture uniquely Hong Kong. The compact

Figure 3
Queen's Road Central, Hong Kong

Figure 4
Cantonese opera, *Red Boat*

high-density living with effective street lives had cultivated community bonds and business synergies as witnessed in the street cultures of Shamshuipo and Wanchai, like electronics stalls along Apliu Street, or wedding-card shops along Lee Tung Street (Figure 5). The mixed-use living plus working conditions were incidentally addressing the issues of commuting as well as community building. They allowed the city to create a possibility of 'compact culture' where convenience and immediacy had overridden other urban values, like formality and hierarchy.

This shifting preference of combining living with working had also reinterpreted the idea of modernity; that is, to localize the Western concept in place where space and time were compressed to optimize the interfaces between human interactions. This perspective on compressing modernity toward efficiency with local pragmatism during this period had laid the foundation for an authentic culture of the region. Due to its celebration of efficiency and can-do spirit, a new urban aesthetic emerged where the co-existence of functionality and imagery was enriching the complexity of modernity.

While the twin-cities of Hong Kong and Macau were creating a new modernity that refreshed the cultural identity of contemporary "Chinese" toward the Western world, the region of the Pearl River Delta remained underdeveloped until the "open-door policy" pronounced by Deng Xiaoping in 1978. This groundbreaking policy had granted overseas Chinese, including those from Hong Kong and Macau, new opportunities to invest in China where Guangdong Province was the testing ground for "socialism with Chinese characteristics." From that moment on, the Mainland cities of the region including Guangzhou, Shenzhen, Dongguang, Zhongshan, and Zhuhai were gaining new momentum to attract capitals, talents, and skills from both colonial cities.

At this stage, the cultural shift was once again from the outer ports (Hong Kong and Macau) to the inner capital (Guangzhou, Shenzhen, and so on), but this time it was a localized modernity brewed for over half a century by the twin-cities instead of any direct Western cultural imposition from Europe. This importation of contemporary culture onto the ready-to-change territories of the Pearl River Delta had dramatically transformed the cultural landscape where new ideas were no longer foreign but familiar.

4. Sovereignty Change

In 1997 and 1999 respectively, the consecutive changes of sovereignty of Hong Kong and Macau had permeated the political barriers between the colonial twin-cities and the Mainland cities with subtle differentiation under the overarching agenda of "one country, two systems." The urban developments onward were shifting gear toward a new trajectory with a bigger picture of "integration." Recharged with new roles from "windows" to "bridges" with leverage of the accrued momentum toward global platforms, both post-colonial cities were taking up unprecedented challenges. As one of the vertices in the global financial triangle, Hong Kong was presuming an equivalence to New York and London forming the 'Nylonkong'[3] (Figure 6) while Macau was elevated from a local gambling hub to an all-round family entertainment empire compatible to Las Vegas (Figure 7). As a result, extensive reclamation projects and mega-scale developments were undertaken at the turn of the century. Massive integrated commercial complexes, like IFC and ICC, were built at strategic reclaimed waterfronts of Victoria Harbour in Hong Kong, and Cotai in Macau, an extensive reclaimed Vegas-like gambling and tourism area aligned with luxurious hotels and casinos.

With an ambition to compete in the global arena, the region is now refueled to release the potential powers through the concept of "Greater China." After forty years of the "open door policy," China as an emerging superpower, the integration of '9+2' cluster cities within the Pearl River Delta is being redefined as "strategic partnership" toward a bigger picture of the Great Bay Area. To synchronize uneven developments in the region is meant to step up the productivity to outbid its counterparts of San Francisco Bay Area and Tokyo Bay Area[4]. With the PRD being re-conceived as the GBA from an economic viewpoint rather than a cultural perspective, different cities are shouldering their individual duties; for example, Hong Kong as the financial platform, Shenzhen as the Silicon Valley, and Macau as the entertainment hub. As these cities are being re-ordered, Hong Kong and Macau in particular are restructuring their past identities from outer towns, colonial cities, and commercial hubs, toward a new identity within the GBA.

5. Interlinking Divergence

With a new definition of the GBA to drive further economic growth, the cultural underlay of the Pearl River Delta enables an assimilation of differences among the other member cities, but at the same time may also react to revert any superimposed alignments. For example, the recently launched Hong Kong-Zhuhai-Macau Bridge[5] is built with the intention to bridge the western and eastern coasts of the PRD. The debate between the "single Y" design as built and the "double-Y" proposal to link Shenzhen is a

Figure 5
"Wedding Card" Street

Figure 6
Nylonkong

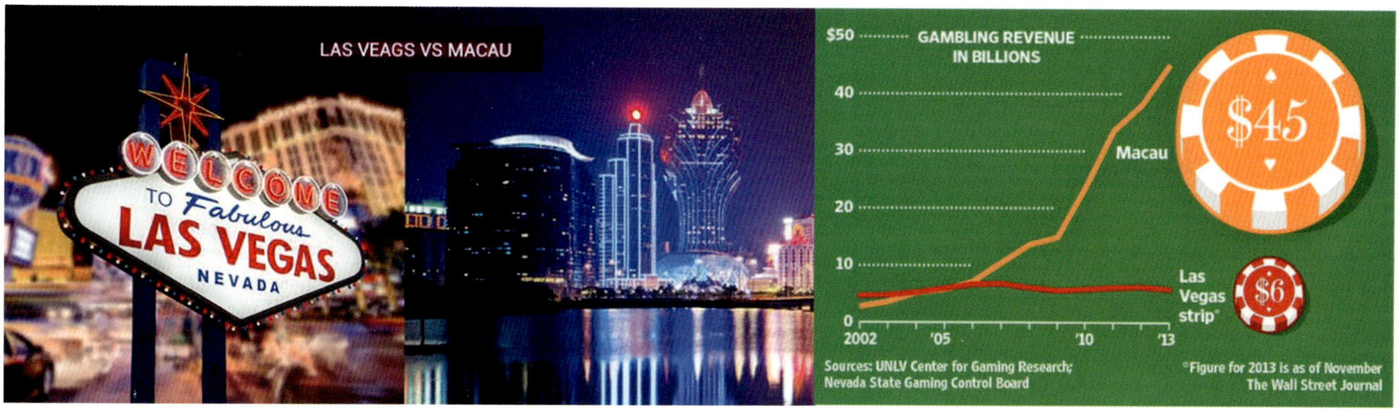

Figure 7
Macau vs Las Vegas

manifestation of the political struggle for economic leadership over the territory. Although Shenzhen, being the fastest developing city attracting talents from all over China, tends to equate its significance with Hong Kong, it is restrained due to its lack of local cultural affiliation. In the aftermath, Shenzhen is finally looking for an alternative bridge connection between the city and the adjacent west-coast city of Zhongshan.

In this regard, the lost "genius loci" latent behind the complex political and historical overlays, now being unveiled through two layers of deliberation from the Beijing government and regional stakeholders, becomes an imminent issue among the cities. Hence, questions are being raised. "Who is the leader of the Great Bay Area?"; "What should be the roles of the two Special Economic Zones?"; "Should Hong Kong and Macau be treated differently from other cluster cities?"; "How should the old cultural capital of Guangzhou and the new techno capital of Shenzhen be positioned?"

Although the cross-pollinated cultures in Hong Kong and Macau have undergone labor pains for over a century, the hybrids based on traditional Cantonese culture are maturing in terms of cultural preferences and value systems to maintain their own uniqueness and reject any imposing ideologies. Seemingly the current regional operation is a skewed relationship for economic benefits over political alignments, thus from time to time, there emerges an ideological crisis whenever the sensitive issue of identity affiliation is being questioned. So, coming back to our earlier question: What makes the minds of people from the PRD cities "think and act together"? The hurdle of thinking together may depend on the level of trust in one another.

6. Competitive Collaboration

The consideration of individual cities for their own benefits depends largely on their economic indicators. By comparing scenarios at the two ends of the spectrum, one being competitors fighting for resources and economic growth, the other being collaborators looking for common goals, it may over-simplify the situation if economy is the sole consideration to explain why these cities are "thinking and acting together." In a sense, the incentive to save redundant material and personnel resources is one reason to gear them together, but more is why they are willing to form the cluster as one of collaboration instead of competition.

The cultural conflicts between Hong Kong and Macau are relatively marginal as they share similar history of colonial cities though ruled by two separate European cultures. The discouragement of using the local dialect of Cantonese in mainstream media or even in daily lives of cities across the border, like Guangzhou, not to mention the new immigrant city of Shenzhen, is leading to a dilution of cultural affiliation to the place. Thus, the displacement of the Pearl River Delta as a cultural domain by the economic entity of the Great Bay Area concept is intentional but also harmful to the organically germinated contemporary culture that tends to blend the global perspective with local understandings.

As reflected in the urban situations of both Hong Kong and Macau, the most admirable and surviving streetscapes still embrace genuine local character. Even though the urban density and living conditions, such as the traditional Chinese urban housing, 'Tonglau', may not be ideal and need improvement, the cultural flavors have germinated inspirations for contemporary movies and designs (Figure 8). In a similar manner, the revived attention to traditional rural villages, like those of Lai Chi Wo and Yim Tin Tsai in the countryside of Hong Kong or Taipa Old Town in Macau, with proper artistic and cultural inputs, is showing a unique humanistic perspective on how local cultures are harmoniously blending both Western and traditional lifestyles.

Figure 8
Genius loci of Hong Kong & Macau

7. Intermixed Hybridity

The readiness to accept different cultures into the contemporary Cantonese-speaking societies of Hong Kong and Macau is forming a self-conscious protection to reject the generic pan-China ideology. When Western visitors could easily seek another familiar cultural environment to intermingle with the local Cantonese speakers, the interpretation of collaboration may deviate from the official intention of regional coordination, but rather it should be an evolving integration of global values with local mindsets.

The phenomenon of cultural mutation to integrate global values with local mindsets is based on the foundation of hybrid cultural genes formed in the colonial period of Hong Kong and Macau, but now at an elevated magnitude to associate with other hybrid cultures that also experienced processes of hybridization. The common aspiration for newness based on pragmatism with local cultural twists is offering a propelling momentum in their cultures. With an unconscious avoidance of dominant traditions, these cultures are offering an opportunity for creativity to blend in their local contexts, like the contemporary culture of "compact modernity" evolved in Hong Kong. Compact living unit designs, like that of Domestic Transformer by Gary Chang or the recent Light

Figure 9
Compact living

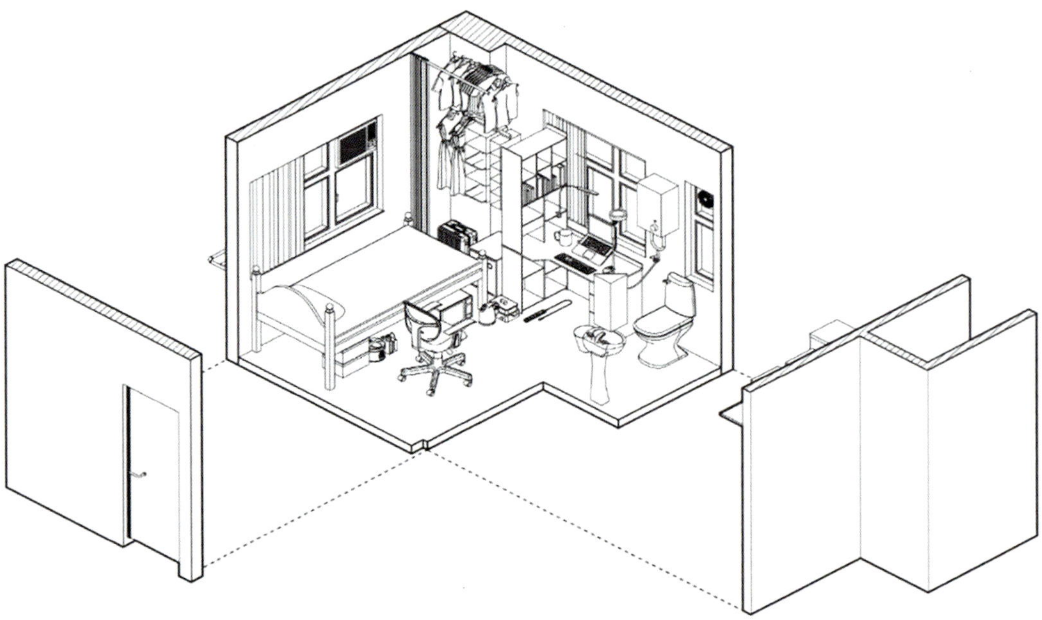

Housing by Housing Bureau, are trying to address contemporary living conditions of limited space and short-term provision with local cultural wisdom (Figure 9).

The emergence of a self-consciousness is setting a new agenda for the region to consider whether the people here should think of themselves as culturally distinct. The development of this thinking has been embedded in the cultural genes to look for newness from the beginning of the Western influences through maritime trading in Macau for over four centuries and Hong Kong over the last two centuries. The spirit of freedom and departing from the traditions and a denial of authoritarianism builds an environment where 'free-space' enables people to look forward. Beyond the political framing of the GBA, people of Hong Kong and Macau are gradually influencing those of the PRD, now looking toward a renewed identity not simply defined by the original Cantonese culture but fueled by their openness to absorb global influences. Together with the manufacturing capacity upon the "open-door policy", the PRD region has accustomed to a mode of production for whatever they are ordered to supply, the same mindset now applicable in the production of culture.

Through external inputs of cultural ingredients, the consciousness of making things happen allows a diversity of cultures to take roots in the region. When these cultural components are recomposed and manufactured into products, the idea of "cultural manufacturing" may come into the picture that by integrating imported cultural elements into a whole becomes a new phenomenon. In this regard, the recent completion of Taipa Casino City in Macau, including Venetian, Parisian, and Londoner elements is a manifestation of how imported cultures, say second-hand interpretations from other cultural capitals, are reinterpreted and deliberately fabricated with a local twist. Equally the West Kowloon Cultural District in Hong Kong, another culture-import project, is meant to position Hong Kong as the Asian cultural capital via "making culture." World-renowned architects are offering their personal touches in "making architecture." to ignite the cultural torches on a piece of reclaimed land without any context. Although there is a subtle understanding of the difference between fabricated and authentic cultures, people of the PRD accept readily the imported cultures as an enriched consumption for their extended cultural appetites.

8. Pragmatic Identity

With this pragmatic openness to absorb and digest imported cultures, the region is not interested in orthodox traditions but an allowance to perceive culture as an evolving way of life for their digested modernity. So, instead of looking for a unified perspective for the GBA to perform coherently, alternatively it may be seeking for a coordinated diversity of relevant cultures with differences. This concerted diversity model is working on a cultural platform with shared values that marginalize the differences. This evolving process is driving the region toward an open unknown future. In this spirit, thus, the 'alternative territory' is the common ground to stimulate and unite people in the PRD. Together they are searching for its contemporary role in the global platform through its interpretative understanding of the region's character. It is probably the key to resolve the uncompromising dilemma of "control" and "freedom" in integrating the '9+2' city clusters as a workable whole. The question, then, is whether the PRD region is ready to produce its own cultural identity beyond its economic achievement or simply subdue itself within the political framing of the GBA?

Without any hardliner to draw the barrier between capitalistic and socialistic territories, Hong Kong and Macau under the "one country, two systems" axiom have been undergoing a dynamic evolution. In fact, for the last two decades the twin-cities have departed further and taken slightly diversified paths toward the opposite ends of the spectrum. At the one end, the path taken by Macau is toward an emphasis on rapid economic growth whereby the remaining self-containing Macanese communities are treated as a specimen of "preserved" culture. By preserving the historic urban center as a UNESCO heritage precinct[6] with due respect to the original hybrid Macanese culture, other mega-developments at the urban fringes are fast-tracking to support the overall economic growth.

At the other end, people of Hong Kong have recognized the urgency to establish a new aspiration for cultural identity. Thus, the introduction of revitalization schemes for heritage conservation of both colonial and traditional buildings has stimulated creativity with community participation for a revived identity with people and place being integrated as an inseparable whole. For example, the revitalization of Tai O Police Station into Tai O Heritage Hotel and Mei Ho House into City Hostel has well illustrated the common desire to recapture the old memory for new identity (Figure 10).

In addition, the urban transformations from the redevelopment of Kai Tak Airport[7], Energizing Kowloon East[8], demonstrate the dynamism in how Hong Kong people capitalize their manufacturing capacity into cultural mutations. For the Kai Tak developments, the area is reviving the idea of arcaded streetscape inherited from the light-industrial urban ensembles in the 1960s to foster neighborhood communications again but this time within a high-rise condition. The Energizing Kowloon East Project under an official agenda is trying to realize "smart city" concepts through revamping the obsolete industrial precincts with fin-tech industries and cultural workforces. It is to reveal the 'Lion Rock Spirit' by transforming the district into an alternative 'CBD', Cultural Brewing District. The driving engine of creativity has thus been taking root through a self-reliant attitude since the manufacturing period of the '60s. This reinterpretation through an introduction of technical innovation and mind-craftsmanship is exploring a localized position with cultural confidence.

9. Cultural Complexity

As an emerging model to spearhead the cultural direction through new means of manufacturing, smart technology and human cohesion, the influence is extending toward the PRD via softer channels of designs, instituted networks, lifestyle inductions and social innovations. So, without any negotiation or compromise on political positions, these soft impacts are creating the third wave toward the PRD population overriding the last two waves of industrializing in the '80s and 'pop-culture washing' in the '90s. The reciprocal impacts between the cultural generators of Hong Kong and the receptive PRD cities are rapidly absorbed through means of frequent daily travelers (commonly known as 'water guests') plus social media as cultural commuters. Once again, the grassroot exchanges of daily life between the reconciled twin-cities and the inland cities, this time through reciprocal flows, are reinforcing their mindscape as "one" but complex.

These complex interpretations of a common aspiration for a contemporary lifestyle synchronizing the effectiveness of modernity with the hybridized spirit are mind-shaped by cultural innovators mostly based in Hong Kong. When the new generations' demand for an open society embracing universal values of freedom and justice is confronting the utilitarian mindset of the previous generations, the inter-generational contradictions are adding complexities to how the twin-cities position themselves for the coming century. Without a simple resolution, it has been taking a non-linear evolving process to re-conceive the region from a pure economic entity toward a hybrid double complex with a bi-axial model of politico-economic and socio-cultural integration.

Along the politico-economic axis, given the asymmetrical developments in the past, if a pragmatic resolution exists, it should be subordinated to the socio-cultural order. With stronger ties through socio-cultural cohesion that has been germinated through a natural growth from the territories' genes of hybrid cultures, it is possible to override the presumed politico-economic alignments. To elevate and recognize the cultural merits accumulated over centuries for their being "alternative" from the formal Chinese culture is the only way to unleash the potentials of the PRD region as a cultural regime supported by its highly coordinated manufacturing, technological, and financial engines.

10. Re-imagined Reality

To resolve these conflicting cultural complexities, "the architecture of the cities" should be the way of thinking. If we revisit the idea from Aldo Rossi's[9] conception of cities, these cities along the Pearl River Delta should share the same founding "genius loci" embedded in the cultural memories of the place, in this case, the blue territories that used to connect people together. These blue territories of open sea and river networks have been building up a cultural character that reflects the dynamic personality of the people. Through the evolution from fishing villages, then entrepots, light industrial communities, to global financial and entertainment hubs, the final destiny of the twin-cities of Hong Kong and Macau is yet to be explored via various cultural means. The common threads are all about their openness toward the world, pragmatic attitude in realizing individual aspirations, and a receptive capacity for integration.

In order to revive this spirit of the place, new attempts from individual cities are being made to redefine local traditions like Cantonese opera through architecture and urban design, as witnessed in the Xiqu Center at West Kowloon District in Hong Kong and Wing Hing Fong at Lychee Bay in Guangzhou. Both projects are interpretations to reinstate the intangible cultural heritage of Cantonese opera but through two approaches. Xiqu Center is meant to elevate the tradition towards an international level by a contemporary expression of an 'unveiling curtain' to suggest a revival through live performance of the art form toward the world while that at Wing Hing Fong being intertwined within the traditional urban fabric is suggesting the integrated experience of art with daily living (Figure 11).

Although there may be imposition of cultural footprints, like the imported Art Basel Hong Kong event and the transplanted Hong Kong Palace Museum from Beijing, these cultural scenes said to embellish the city can hardly be rooted as natural outgrowths of its true spirit. On the other hand, the city is still maintaining a local

Figure 10
Revitalization of Tai O Police Station within the community

Figure 11
Xiqu Center and Wing Hing Fong

flavor of creativity in urban communities where relevant traditions along the water-bodies are still practiced and reinterpreted. The recent revival of the waterways of Lychee Bay Scenic Area of Guangzhou and Kai Tak River of Hong Kong are counterparts in the PRD to re-examine how the human landscape may recall the community culture associated with the waterways in the post-industrial landscape (Figure 13). The approaches are similar but the interpretations on the cultural heritage may span between these cities' preferences. In the case on Lychee Bay, the urban intervention initiated by the local government reopens a paved channel to reconnect historical relics where the waterway suggests a revisit to the city's history. In the Kai Tak River, an alternative approach, advocated for over a decade by the author, was taken where the concept of 'future memory' is implemented. The recharged waterway is to bring about imaginations for the future generations upon their understanding of the past that is only partially remembered. Together with the socio-ecological integration, the revived waterway will bring about further lively inputs from senior to junior citizens.

In this sense, the possible construct of dreams upon realities is empowering a new global citizenship that helps further the evolution of the cultural heritage in place. This provision of an open environment for memories and imaginations is, in fact, a tangential reality of the presence that keeps the evolutionary momentum of the culture rolling. As the current challenge of the GBA perspective is suggesting new insights into the PRD's cultural identity, this provides a wider spectrum to see cultural citizenship beyond the local territory toward a new horizon. Given the solid foundation of economic support and synchronized minds, maybe it is time to reshape this region from the past role of digesting imported cultures to a new role of exporting contemporary cultural ideas through the Water Silk Road.

Notes

1. '9+2', a general term referring to the cluster of cities in the Great Bay Area, including nine Mainland cities of Guangzhou, Shenzhen, Zhuhai, Foshan, Huizhou, Dongguan, Zhongshan, Jiangmen, and Zhaoqing, plus two Special Administrative Regions of Hong Kong and Macau.
2. 'Great Bay Area', the Outline Development Plan for the Guangdong-Hong Kong-Macao Greater Bay Area promulgated on 18 February 2019. https://www.bayarea.gov.hk/en/focus/bayarea-cities.html.
3. 'Nylonkong', a contraction of New York-London-Hong Kong, first appeared in *Time* magazine in 2008; the article suggests that the cities share similarities, especially in being globalized financial and cultural centers, and are the most remarkable cities in the 21st century. https://en.wikipedia.org/wiki/Nylonkong.
4. 'Bay Areas', a comparable statistic data of the three Bay Areas at 2018: Great Bay Area—the total population is over 71 million, the GDP is USD 1,642.5 billion and GDP per capita is USD 23,342; San Francisco Bay Area—the total population is over 9.7 million, the GDP is USD 1,031.9 billion and GDP per capita is USD 106,757; Tokyo Bay Area—the total population is over 38 million, the GDP is USD 1,759 billion and GDP per capita is USD 46,289.
5. 'Hong Kong-Zhuhai-Macau Bridge'(HZMB), opened on 6 February 2018, is a 55-kilometer bridge-tunnel system consisting of a series of three cable-stayed bridges, an undersea tunnel, and four artificial islands. It is both the longest sea crossing and the longest open-sea fixed link on earth. The HZMB spans the Lingding and Jiuzhou channels, connecting Hong Kong, Macau, and Zhuhai—three major cities on the Pearl River Delta. https://en.wikipedia.org/wiki/Hong_Kong%E2%80%93Zhuhai%E2%80%93Macau_Bridge.
6. 'UNESCO heritage precinct': the inscribed property presents a group of 22 principal buildings and public spaces that enable a clear understanding of the structure of the old trading port city. With its historic streets, residential, religious, and public Portuguese and Chinese buildings, the Historic Center of Macau provides a unique testimony to the meeting of aesthetic, cultural, religious, architectural, and technological influences from East and West. It bears witness to the first and most enduring encounter between China and the West, based on the vibrancy of international trade. https://whc.unesco.org/en/list/1110/.
7. Kai Tak was always so much more than an airport. Hong Kong's iconic international travel hub played a pivotal role in metropolitan life for 73 years, which came to an end with its closure 20 years ago. And rather than being marooned on the urban fringe like many busy aviation facilities, the airport was poised cheek by jowl with a residential neighborhood and thousands of Kowloon City residents could not help but be aware of the precise moments the runway opened and closed. https://www.scmp.com/magazines/post-magazine/long-reads/article/2153099/remembering-kai-tak-hong-kong-airport-closed-20.

8 'Energizing Kowloon East': the project takes this pilot area to explore the feasibility of

Figure 12
Lychee Bay Scenic Area and Kai Tak River

developing a smart city. It has been proactively engaging stakeholders including government departments, public utility companies, public transport operators, IT sector, academic, and research institutions to exchange ideas for seeking collaboration opportunities to push ahead with this policy initiative. https://www.ekeo.gov.hk/en/smart_city/index.html.
9. In the book *The Architecture of the City* (MIT Press, 1982), Aldo Rossi held that the city remembers its past (our "collective memory") and through this as the reference to rediscovery of the traditional European city. The same idea may be applicable in the rediscovery of the PRD cities.

Figure Credits
Figure 1: PRD Vs GBA in 1979 & 2019 (Author's photo-collage)
Figure 2: Water-borne communities along the Pearl River Delta (Courtesy of Lai Fong)
Figure 3: Queen's Road Central, Hong Kong (Courtesy of iStock: Getty Images)
Figure 4: Cantonese Opera, *Red Boat* (Courtesy of Zoonar/Leung Cho Pan: Alamy)
Figure 5: "Wedding Card" Street (Courtesy of Dr. Mark Greene)
Figure 6: Nylonkong, global financial triangle, New York, London, and Hong Kong (Courtesy of Time Inc.)
Figure 7: Macau Vs Las Vegas (Courtesy of Jose Javier Zarza, UNLV Center for Gaming Research, Nevada State Gaming Research Board)
Figure 8: Genius loci of Hong Kong and Macau (Courtesy of Steven Wei: Unsplash)
Figure 9: Compact living (Courtesy of HKU BAAS Yr 1 Studio)
Figure 10: Revitalization of Tai O Police Station within the community (Courtesy of Hong Kong Lands Department)
Figure 11: Xiqu Center Vs Wing Hing Fong (Courtesy of Ema Peter: Wallpaper, PQ77wd: Wikipedia)
Figure 12: Lychee Bay Scenic Area Vs Kai Tak River (Author's photo-collage)

ARTICLE

The Local and the Multiplicity of Chinese Architecture

WANG Jun-yang, School of Architecture and Urban Planning, Nanjing University

Abstract

This paper investigates the theme of local construction against the background of the quest for overall disciplinary knowledge and indigenous architecture in the twentieth-century Chinese architectural discourse. It proceeds with the ideas of local knowledge in terms of *feng-tu*, climate, and material/technique as three fundamentals for local construction. It calls for a Chinese architecture predicated on local multiplicities.

Author Information
WANG Jun-yang: wangjunyang@nju.edu.cn

Keywords

Local construction, the multiplicity of Chinese architecture, the twentieth-century Chinese architectural discourse

If it is accepted that Chinese architecture as a discipline, beginning with the first generation of Chinese architects who studied abroad at the beginning of the twentieth century, has since been maturing thanks to the efforts of the following generations, then it can be said that more than a century has witnessed the development of modern Chinese architecture and all the buildings along with it. Two themes seem to have loomed large over times, which could be identified as *Ben-ti* (本体), to be understood as disciplinary knowledge, and *Ben-tu* (本土), translated as indigenous architecture in this essay.

1. From *Ben-ti* and *Ben-tu* to the Local

Both the terms *Ben-ti* and *Ben-tu* are relatively new. At the early stage of modern Chinese architecture, *Ben-ti* was largely ratified by a classical theory known as "architecture is the combination of science and arts,"[1] while *Ben-tu* was basically linked to the so-called National Style of Chinese Architecture. Yet, we know now that, if the term *Ben-ti* is to have any significance and hold, it must be understood as disciplinary knowledge rather than architecture itself. In the tradition of Western architecture, since the Renaissance, such disciplinary knowledge was long considered universal, and eventually called forth a theory of composition that prevailed in the academy, often without concerning itself with regional and cultural differences. None is perhaps more striking in this regard than *Eléments et theorie de l'architecture* by Julien Guadet, professor of architectural theory at École nationale supérieure des beaux-arts, Paris, France, in the nineteenth century.

In the English world, composition was brought into architectural terminology in association with the request for Picturesque, in which free and asymmetrical organizations were explored. It was, however, the growing demand for character during the rise of Romanticism that finally led to the collapse of the universal value of academic tradition. Colin Rowe, an architectural historian and theorist of the twentieth century once observed, "If the academic tradition has been preoccupied with the ideal and with its physical embodiment as a visual norm; (and) had promulgated laws and had been indisposed to concern itself with exceptions with these," it is because it holds that "the whole beauty and grandeur of art consists in being able to get above all singular forms, local customs, particularities and details of every kind." Yet for Romanticism, it was all the paradoxical accidents inherent in the latter that was just "full of interest and 'character' ".[2] It was, as Rowe concluded, "the fundamental demand which typifies the architecture of the nineteenth century."[3]

Romanticism's demand for character called for both "artistic character" and "local character." If the former was a matter of artistic personality, then the latter had to do with the ethos of a nation-state on one hand, and the atmosphere or mode of a specific place on the other. In Romanticism, Gothic architecture was furthermore considered an incarnation of national characteristics both in England and in Germany, or Prussia as it was known at that time. Interestingly, this was the situation even in France, where classicism reached its apotheosis. That means, if classicism gave rise to a France in the universal sense, then Gothic stood for the indigenous France. Apart from that, the notion of character was closely linked to the specific location and atmosphere of a building. That is to say, whether in the countryside or on the shore of the sea, or with a wide view or next to a river, or in the mountains or woods, the building should in its best way reveal the character of the location accordingly[4]—hence the local, as an architectural issue of significance.

In twentieth century China, Liang Suu-ch'eng (梁思成) was known for his fundamental contribution to the understanding and history of Chinese architecture. It is agreed among contemporary scholars that Liang's idea was primarily shaped by the Beaux-Arts education that he received at the University of Pennsylvania in the United States—so was the *Reference Portfolio for Architectural Design* (建筑设计参考图集) compiled by Liang and his co-workers from the 1930s on, to the extent that the Reference Portfolio was initially prepared for designing the National Style of Chinese Architecture. One might say, it reconciled the composition theory of the academic system and the seemingly opposing concept of character at one stroke on the nationalistic level.

It was at this juncture that Liang expressed his dissatisfaction with the writings on Chinese architecture by Chuta Ito (伊东忠太), a Japanese architectural scholar, and Osvald Siren, a Swedish sinologist and art historian. For Liang, their work either "failed to get to the heart of the matter" because of "the lack of studies of buildings themselves," or "was unable to outline the essence of Chinese architecture" due to "the deficient knowledge of the structural system and historical evolution of Chinese architecture." As to Yue Jiazao's (乐嘉藻) *A History of Chinese Architecture* (中国建筑史)—the first output of this genre by Chinese writers—Liang disproved it on the ground that it was more "personal notes or essays" rather than a "history."[5]

As some present scholars have pointed out, Liang's interpretation and narration of architectural history seemed to have been inseparable from the stimulus of Sir Banister Fletcher's *A History of Architecture*, a standard work that Liang got exposed to during his time at the University of Pennsylvania. The commitment that Liang set for himself was one that was set on figuring out the characteristics and the historical evolution of Chinese architecture in an attempt to respond to, or rather to counteract, Fletcher's "A Tree of Architecture" diagram in which the evolution of Wester architecture was depicted as a "historical style," while Chinese architecture—together with Indian, Persian or Mexican—was relegated to a "non-historical style."[6] Denouncing Fletcher's thesis, yet borrowing its historical framework, Liang's outline of the historical evolution of Chinese architecture aimed to demonstrate that it could be equally legitimated as a sophisticated "historical style," just as Western architecture was. He even used biological metaphor to describe its historical trajectory, saying, "The Chinese building is a highly 'organic' structure. It is an indigenous growth that (was) conceived and born in the remote prehistoric past, reached its 'adolescence' in the Han dynasty (around the beginning of the Christian era), matured into full glory and vigor in the Tang dynasty (seventh and eighth centuries), mellowed with grace and elegance in the Song dynasty (eleventh and twelfth centuries), then started to show signs of old age, feebleness, and rigidity, from the beginning of the Ming dynasty (fifteenth century)."[7]

Yet this is only part of the story. The other part is Liang's pursuit of the "grammar" and the "vocabulary" of Chinese architecture that he believed could be used in design practice. To this end, grammar was most primal, while vocabularies indispensable. As Liang noted: "To get on Chinese architecture, one should learn its 'grammar' first, and command its rules and regulations." This would necessarily involve knowledge of the structural carpentry (大木作) of Chinese architecture ranging from the articulation of all groups of *Tou-kung* (斗栱)(the bracket set) to the whole structural system ... which served as the grammar of Chinese architecture. Other elements of non-strunctural carpentry (小木作) as well as color painting would work in the same way as words and vocabularies in verbal sentences."[8] This led Liang to designate *Ying-Tsao-Fa-Shih* (营造法式), a treatise on architecture dating from 1103 in the Song dynasty, and *Kung-Cheng-Tso-Fa* (工程做法), the official regulations for architecture in the Qing dynasty published by the Ministry of Works in 1733, as "two grammar books" on Chinese architecture. Joined by collaborators from the Society for the Study of Chinese Architecture, and through dedicating pursuits to the field studies of surviving buildings from the past while also consulting the craftsmen who maintained the traditional knowledge and skills, Liang succeeded not only in decoding those two classical works, but most importantly, in laying the foundation for "the historical construction of Chinese architecture and the explanation of its architectural system."[9] It is now widely held that herein lies Liang's greatest contribution to modern Chinese architecture.

One should not miss out, however, certain polemics raised on such "historical construction" and "architectural system." Among them the most challenging one came from Han Pao-teh (汉宝德), a Taiwan based scholar in architectural history and theory. Han wrote: "Our country, a unified empire titled as the Celestial Dynasty, has always favored orthodoxy. Centered on the imperial capital, it considers the development of remote areas insignificant. Such view is shared among intellectuals growing up with the examination and appointment system centered on the imperial capital."[10] As a counter argument, Han spoke of an awareness of the South. The fact that the South, after Song and Yuan reign, stood out as the center of Chinese culture, Han argued, turns the theory of the "declining" of the Ming and the Qing architecture disprovable. For him, "it would be unreasonable to talk about a declining architecture in the region that was culturally prosperous. Nothing was more convincing in this respect than the highlight of garden art in the South during the Ming and the Qing times."[11] Moreover, as the literati in the South strove for spiritual liberty and abandoned the formalized and rigid style of court painting in favor of the lyrical expression of the splendid natural landscapes of Jiangnan region, the Jiangnan architecture of the Ming time was keen on something new beyond the formalized rigidity of the court standards, looking for change in accordance with natural condition and landscapes. "Where the architectural rigidity of the magnificent palaces in the North was dominant, there was the vivid adaptation to local and natural conditions in the South." Or, as it is often said in another way, "While the North respects laws, the South is (in) favor of conditions."[12] To a great extent, one might say, this is the source for architectural deviation and diversity in the South, let alone the fact that many of the so-called "monuments" in the South are made without the system of *Tou-kung*, or *Dou-gong* as it is now spelled.

It must be said that Han's critique is not to be turned down on the ground that—as it is sometimes argued—Liang and his co-workers started their work on the so-called vernacular buildings in Shanxi Province in as early as the 1930s, not to mention the fact that the southeastern branch of the Society for the Study of Chinese Architecture did engage itself with similar studies from 1938 to 1945—meaning, what Han's critique targeted was an already established historical system of Chinese architecture rather than the growing history of research around it. It seems that, however, Han did not offer any historically significant conclusion out of the polemic. Instead, it was Chen Zhihua (陈志华), a scholar in architectural history and theory, based at Tsinghua University in Beijing, who in a review on Han's "Two Points on the Ming and the Qing Architecture" (明、清建筑二论) delivered observations with historical consequences which Liang's quest for a "history" probably called for. In Chen's observation, the deviation of the Ming architecture in the South from the official orthodoxy in the North was effectively a product of the "rudimentary stage of capitalist development." And "moving away from the feudalistic orthodoxy, such architectural development activated a historical progress leading to the virtue of the architecture of the Ming and the Qing dynasties."[13]

Given Chen's enthusiasm for the "Marxist" tradition of history, one is hardly astonished by such remarks. What is more relevant for the theme here, nevertheless, is another observation of Chen claiming that "if it is accepted that Ming and Qing architecture in the South is historically more significant than the official one in the North, the current system of architectural history of the period would await change. The same holds true to the whole system of architecture history if the locality and ethnicity of Chinese architecture is considered. So far, the historical system of Chinese architecture has been recorded in sequence of dynasties following the system of *Twenty-Four Books of History*, in which each period is comprised of the same components: cities, palaces, temples, dwellings, and so on. Local and ethnical dimension and ways of life have yet to be included. One can even go so far as to say that local architectural studies have not been started." On top of that, "the current historical system of Chinese architecture is largely Han ethnic oriented, apart from (being) official system oriented. As such, it tends to lock out historical investigations that are very much needed for our time. Unless such a system is broken, no breakthrough could be expected in the historiography of Chinese architecture. Its expansion means no more than the assembly of more source material."[14]

Chen was probably referring to "minority ethnic groups" other than Han in the above. And it seems that in Chen's argument, if "locality" seems to be different from "ethnicity," they may mean the same as well. Anyhow, given the fact that studies of ethnically vernacular architecture have become an important part of the history of Chinese architecture over the last decades—involving large number of villages and towns, residential buildings, gardens, decorations, religious buildings, ethnic buildings, and others—what has resulted from it so far seems to only consolidate Chen's argument, while the "breakthrough" in the historical system of Chinese architecture that Chen called for still seems to remain remote.

2. The Local and Local Knowledge

In such context, the local and local construction are two issues worth exploring. That which is local, and the differences and diversities that tag along with it are omnipresent. More importantly, the understanding of the local requires "local knowledge" to use the notion introduced by American anthropologist Clifford Geertz. This notion was deployed as the title of an anthology concerning "interpretive anthropology," but it was not until the last essay entitled "Local Knowledge: Fact and Law in Comparative Perspective" that Geertz's idea on local knowledge became explicit. By studying the judicial systems in Morocco, Bali and Java, Geertz made fascinating accounts of the role that local knowledge plays to the judicial system and juridical interpretations in the context of—respectively—Islam, Hinduism, and a hybrid religious culture.

We cannot go into Geertz's juristic topic of course. What can be said on this connection is that Geertz's initiation has since evoked a range of thoughts on the relationship between local knowledge and universal knowledge. As Ye Shuxian, a contemporary Chinese writer and scholar of humanities, observed in his highly cited essay titled "On Local Knowledge": the hermeneutic anthropological tendency to take on "local knowledge" formed from the view point of cultural relativism has offered vivid ideas from both within and outside the discipline. And "by looking at Western cultures and societies from the cultural perspective of 'the Other,' more and more anthropologists have now realized that (the) Western knowledge system, traditionally considered and legitimized as universal and normative criterion, is effectively a man-made 'construct' and is no more valid than 'local knowledge' under given circumstances." Opposed to conventional beliefs, therefore, "it is now widely accepted that 'local knowledge' not only has every reason to be on a par with universal knowledge but is (also) irreplaceable because of its enormous potentials as a form of human perception."[15]

That local knowledge is not only complementary to universal knowledge but could also surpass, and even serve, as a critique of the latter brings to mind the argument of Michel Foucault in his *Les mots et les choses*. Foucaul's point of argument is that throughout the times, the system of knowledge has always presented itself as a reflection of the order of things—hence the English version of the book title: *The Order of Things*. The two ruptures in Western culture since the sixteenth century depicted in the book—one from the Renaissance to the Classical era in the mid-seventeenth century and the other from the Classical era to the modern era at the beginning of the nineteenth century—are examples of this. Interestingly, Foucault suggests that he came to the idea of the book based on the mode of categorization in a "Chinese encyclopedia," informed, and in fact invented, by the Argentine poet and writer Jorge Luis Borges. Disordered as it may seem, such categorization contains for Foucault the possibility of "other spaces," or "hétérotopies," to use Foucault's own terminology. For Claude Levi-Strauss, a French thinker and cultural anthropologist, whose groundbreaking work came into its own a few years prior to Foucault, it is a system of knowledge that grows out of the savage mind, or "la pensée sauvage" as Levi-Strauss put it in French.

This brings us back to the scathing review of Yue Jiazao's *A History of Chinese Architecture* by Liang Suu-ch'eng. What is remarkable with Yue's work is that "roof construction" and "garden buildings" are put together to form a twin topic composing the first part of the book. This is a categorization that Liang found "puzzling," which together with other shortcomings, ultimately led to his "repudiation" of Yue's work. Arguably, Yue's categorization of Chinese architecture was not evident enough as an outcome of "the savage mind" since it was very much likely that—as a recent study noticed—Yue's arrangement of the book grew out of the assumption that "roof" and "garden building" were the two most distinct features of Chinese architecture, particularly in comparison with its counterpart in the West.[16] It is safe to say, however, that in the twentieth century, in Chinese architecture, there does appear that there had been a growing awareness that what had been commonly referred to as vernacular, or *feng-tu*, was seen as something born out of "the savage mind," whether in form of their occurrence, evolution, transformation, or in terms of their site selection, layout, composition, and construction.

It follows that all "the wild ways" of doing things, particularly in rural China, and going beyond the official system tends to give rise to some challenging questions and challenges for academic studies. Is "vernacular" in architecture equal to "residential buildings" or even a single residence? Can "vernacular" include roads, canals, greenery, accesses, gates, wells, ancestral halls and pagodas? The answer is yes, according to existing academic doctrines and guidelines. Yet "we have a feeling that it still does not fit well with the existing categories, which is the reason that we prefer to refer to our research settlement studies by anything other than vernacular architecture studies; and this would include investigations of such materials as local historical documents and photos, and also population numbers, discounted prices of old wooden components, and even remuneration for labor work. It would seem that the time has now come for the study of architecture to let economic, ecological, demographic, and social factors become game changers, transforming the "ego" or, one might say, the "disciplinary bias" of the profession in term of either "composition" or "design concept," and enforce the transition from the "rational thought" of our "cultural being" to that of "savage mind."[17] It is encouraging, therefore, to see a series of research projects and field studies by the settlement group of the former Center for Architectural Studies at Peking University; that their unique way of investigation and presentation will hopefully contribute to a better understanding of those architectural traditions now collectively called the vernacular.

Arguably, the enthusiasm for the thought of "the savage mind" could be easily denounced as "anti-scientific" or "anti-intellectual" by those who are used to "scientific rationality." Similar critiques could be targeted toward the engagement with local knowledge and related epistemological methods. It is not surprising, for example, to see that "hermeneutic anthropology is sometimes accused of lacking in foresight, reproducibility, and verifiability, as well as lacking the ability to form laws. Others blame it for "openly engaging in occult activity," and still others equate it with subjectivism and solipsism, or far extreme relativism."[18] That said, however, it should be noted that neither local knowledge nor the thought of "the savage mind" are to be justified or rejected as complete oppositions to universal knowledge. The virtue of local knowledge, to say the least, resides in the fact that it can offer us tests on the validity of universal knowledge, not to mention the potentials in serving to help break through the limits of universal knowledge.

3. Three Elements of Local Construction

If local construction requires local knowledge, what are the other barometers that can inform both, apart from the "savage mind"? I would like to suggest three interrelated issues in an attempt to address this question: First, *Feng-tu* (风土), and by saying that I am not having in mind what is normally identified as "vernacular architecture" in the first instance, but rather that of "natural conditions and folk customs" in a broader sense. China's records of *Feng-tu* go back a very long time, varying from *The Book of Songs* (诗经), dating from around 600 BC, to a range of documents, of which the earliest well-known one is "The Land and Social Conditions of Yangxian" (阳羡风土记) by Zhou Chu (周处). Other classics include *Jinzhou Record* by Sheng Hongzhi (盛弘之), *Record of Buddhist Temples in Luoyang* (洛阳迦蓝记) by Yang Xuanzhi (杨衒之) and *Record on Custom and Land of Guilin* (桂林风土记) by Mo Xiufu (莫休符). Etymologically, *Feng-tu* consists of *feng* (风) and *tu* (土), of which *feng* literally means the wind, but practically has been used to refer to folk customs and human culture including historical figures, songs, legends and religions, while *tu*, the earth, indicates the natural environment in terms of geography, climate and products nurturing all living things. Or in the words of the ancient Chinese dictionary *Shuowen Jiezi* (说文解字): "*Tu*, the earth that gives birth to everything." Put together, "*Feng-tu*" is "the organic unity of geography and customs, as well as the integration of natural environment and humanistic cultures."[19]

In a work entitled *Fudo*, which is the Japanese equivalent of *Feng-tu*, the Japanese scholar Watsuji Tetsuro defined the whole concept in a similar way: "I use our word *Fudo*, which means literally, 'Wind and Earth,' as a general term for the natural environment of a given land, its climate, its weather, the geological and productive nature of the soil, (and) its topographic and scenic features."[20] This was followed by his classification of the global *Fudo* into three types: "Monsoon," "Desert," and "Meadow;" China and Japan belong to the first one. Here, Watsuji's intention was, as he announced himself, to elaborate on the role played by *Fudo* in shaping people's lifestyles, cultural activities, and even national characters—East and South Asia, Africa and Mongolia, and Europe and the West.

To a certain extent, one must say, Watsuji has achieved his goal, but his theory still seemed imbued with carting difficulties, to the extent that it is too general to be relevant in many instances. For example, although sharing the type of Monsoon, Chinese, and Japanese cultures are so vastly different, let alone their differences with that of South Asia that, according to Watsuji, falls into the very same type of Monsoon as well. Talking about the link between the differences of "the local" and artistic characteristics, his claim that "the smaller the 'the local' divisions, the more intricate the details of form that come in question; the broader such divisions, the deeper the insight into artistic character"[21] seems less convincing too. That means, while Watsuji's assumption remains seminal, it needs to be flashed out with more specific conditions of the local rather than general categories of type so as to be practically valid. For the very same reason, one might say Han Pao-teh's division between the North and South could run into the same problem. Despite that, as the translator of the Chinese edition of *Fudo* has pointed out, Watsuji is correct in saying that natural *Fudo* can be transformed into a historical one, and they will keeping interacting with each other. Or as the saying goes, "history is the history of *Fudo*, and *Fudo* is the *Fudo* imbued with history."[22] The same must hold true when it comes to the issue of cultural dissemination, a process that is often believed could happen without necessarily being connected to "the local."

Feng-tu is perhaps best described by literature these days, and we have good reason to see literature as a particular form of local knowledge in our time. As it comes to architecture, I would like to emphasize yet another aspect of local knowledge in relation to *Feng-tu*. As noted before, local knowledge can hardly make claim for itself the validity any where and any time. In the view of anthropologists, however, such local knowledge is often more valid or real than universal knowledge, given local conditions. Besides, such local knowledge is also associated with "goodness" in terms of local socio-cultural appropriateness.[23] In fact, for an architecture of use, whether for religious rituals or for the purpose of everyday life, l knowledge is something that we cannot do without. It is for that reason also the foremost requirement of a good local construction.

Speaking of architecture of use, let's take climate into account as the second element of local construction. Interestingly, when Geoffrey Bownas, a British scholar, translated Watsuji's *Fudo* into English, he named the book *A Climate: A Philosophical Study*. Bownas' use of "climate" refers, obviously, to the natural or physical, as well as humanistic, historical, and religious ones. In this sense, "climate" is equal to *Fudo*. Taking climate as the second element of local construction, however, the intention here is to emphasize the significance of climate as a physical factor in a manner reminiscent of *The Architecture of Well-tempered Environment* by Reyner Banham. We are not supposed, of course, to repeat Banham's theory as a whole, but to look for a reviving of the "selective mode," which in Banham's argument appeared surpassed by the "regenerative mode" of the technology of mechanical means. What is at stake is a matter of translating the "ecological wisdom" of traditional local construction into contemporary design. In contemporary architectural terminology, it becomes a matter of "bioclimatic design," aimed at using wind, heat, sunlight, humidity, and rain as meteorological parameters of architecture. This is to be done through proper building materials, greenery, and landscape design, as well as proper building forms, along with all of its spatial and climatic consequences. The purpose is not only to reduce, if certainly not to eliminate altogether, the use of mechanical or technological means, but to explore human bodily sensations as "meteorological elements and conditions" in both psychophysical and biological domains.[24]

I look forward to seeing more practice of this kind in contemporary Chinese architecture. For an example of international forerunners in this respect, let me give some words to the SESC Pompéia Community Center in São Paulo, Brazil, by the Italian-Brazilian architect Lina Bo Bardi Albeit—a project that is normally regarded as a good example of renovating industrial heritage. Recent studies have shown that Bo Bardi was primarily committed to a more climatic design, and that was not only to deal with the problem caused by an extremely limited budget of the project. Rather, it was as an expression of her female sensitivity which, arguably, seems in strong contrast to the language of *béton brut* that characterized the tower building of this project, that Bo Bardi embraced "atmosphere" in the effort to activate the link between human life predicated on meteorological factors and conditions, and to achieve "a living organism," as Bo Bardi herself said.[25] By inheriting the Brazilian tradition of "bio-climatic modernism" in a modern metropolis, the SESC Pompéia Community Center stands out as an excellent case in which Bo Bardi's critical stance to the "universality" of modern architecture in favor of "the local" is clearly demonstrated.

The third element of local construction involves the issues of materials, structures, and construction techniques. Since the rise of "tectonic culture," which was introduced to Chinese architecture around 2000, these issues have been widely reflected and practiced by Chinese architects, not least by the projects included in this issue of *Architecture Asia*. Given the space limitation of the present essay, we would better allow these projects to speak for themselves.

4. Concluding Remarks

To wrap up, let's say that, whether local construction is taken as a theme of architectural history and theory, or as an issue of contemporary architectural practice, what we need to do today is to drop out style and formal revivalism on the one hand, and grand narrative of a single culture on the other in order to arrive at the multiplicity of Chinese architecture predicated on historical and contemporary conditions of the local.

Notes

1. Li Haiqing, *Modern Transition of Chinese Architecture* (Nanjing: Southeast University Press, 2004), 300.
2. Colin Rowe, "Character and Composition or Some Vicissitudes of Architectural Vocabulary in the Nineteenth Century," *The Mathematics of the Ideal Villa and Other Essays* (Cambridge, Massachusetts and London, England: The MIT Press, 1976), 67.
3. ibid, 80.
4. ibid, 63, 66.
5. Liang Sicheng, "Refutation of Fallacies of Yue Jaizao's A History of Chinese Architecture," *Liang Sicheng The Complete Works Volume 2* (Beijing: China, Architecture Publishing & Media Co., Ltd., 2001), 291.
6. Lai Delin, "Indication of the Subtleties in Liang Sicheng and Lin Huiyin's Writing on History of Chinese Architecture," *Studies in Modern Chinese Architectural History* (Beijing: Tsinghua University Press, 2007), 323.
7. Liang Sicheng, *A Pictorial History of Chinese Architecture, A Bilingual Edition*. translated by Liang Congjie (Tianjin: Baihua Literature And Art Publishing House, 2001), 65-66.
8. Liang Sicheng, "Two 'Grammar Textbooks' of Chinese Architecture," *Bulletin of the Society for Research in Chinese Architecture*, vol. 7, no. 2 (1945): 1-8.
9. Wang Guixiang, "Historical Construction of Chinese Architecture and Explanations on Chinese Architectural System—Two Main Academic Ideals and Contributions of the Society for Research in Chinese Architecture and Liang Sicheng," *Architectural Journal*, no. 12 (2019): 1-6.
10. Han Pao-teh, *Two Arguments on Chinese Architectures in Ming and Qing Dynasties; Origins and Development of Dougong* (Beijing: SDX Joint Publishing Company, 2014).
11. ibid, 12.
12. ibid, 13.
13. Chen Zhihua, "Reviews on Two Points on the Ming and the Qing Architecture," *Dushu*, no. 1 (1991): 108.
14. ibid, 114.
15. Ye Shuxian, "Local Knowledge," *Dushu*, no. 5 (2001): 121-125.
16 Zhang Fan, "The Study on Yue Jiazao's Chinese Architectural History," *Journal of Chinese Architecture History*, no. 4 (2011): 341.
17. Shan Qide, "Vernacular Dwellings and 'Savage Mind'—Reflections on the Academic. Research of Chinese Folk House," *Architectural Journal*, no. 3 (1995): 15.
18. ibid, 19.
19. Li Chuanjun, *Travel Writings of the Han and Tang Dynasties* (Beijing: China Social Sciences Press, 2015), 2-3.
20. Tetsuro Watsuji, *Fudo*, translated by Chen Liwei (Beijing: The Commercial Press, 2020), 4.
21. ibid, 178.
22. ibid, 111.
23. Wu Tong, "A View of Local Knowledge in Philosophy of Scientific Practices," *Study on Local Knowledge*, edited by Ju Shier & Liu Bing (Beijing: The Commercial Press, 2021), 48-49.
24. Silvia Benedito, *Atmosphere Anatomies: On Design, Weather, and Sensation* (Zurich: Lars Müller Publishers, 2021), 17-33.
25. ibid, 216.

Herbalism: A Trend in Contemporary Chinese Architecture

QING Feng, School of Architecture, Tsinghua University

Abstract

This article aims to articulate an important trend in contemporary Chinese architecture through the concept of "Herbalism." First, starting from Kenneth Frampton's interpretation of contemporary Chinese architecture, it points out the inadequacy of understanding contemporary architecture in terms of modern-traditional confrontation. Thereafter, it analyzes the main architectural connotations of Herbalism and illustrates them with corresponding architectural examples. Finally, this article further discusses the philosophical essence of Herbalism, as well as its contemporary value with reference to Martin Heidegger's later philosophy.

Author Information
Qing Feng: Qingfeng@tsinghua.edu.cn

Keywords

China, contemporary architecture, Herbalism, tradition, Spring

Contemporary Chinese architecture has become an integral part of the global architectural scene, characterized by the emergence of a plethora of innovative works of outstanding design quality. How can these works be understood and conceptualized? Is there any common characteristic among them? If so, in what manner do they correlate with China's distinctive cultural traditions? These questions are perhaps the most challenging in architectural research in China. To answer them, this article suggests that the notion of "Herbalism," which has its origin in traditional Chinese medicine (TCM), and which embodies the enduring principles of ancient Chinese philosophy, can be used to signify an important trend in contemporary Chinese architecture. To facilitate further discussion, we will start by examining Kenneth Frampton's view on Chinese contemporary architecture.

1. An interpretation

In the newly published fifth edition of *Modern Architecture: A Critical History*, Frampton dedicates one section to the development of Chinese architecture in recent times, in particular, to architectural practice after the reform and opening-up of China. His main argument is that the development of contemporary Chinese architecture can be summarized as a process of destruction-restoration. He wrote: "Endorsing Wang Shu's reaction against the wanton destruction of China's traditional urban and architectural culture, a new generation of Chinese architects have opted to work in relatively remote rural communities in search of another kind of modernity." Such interpretation presents modern development and Chinese tradition as two sides of a mutual confrontation. The disorderly expansion of the former has brought about a series of problems and even crises. So, some architects turn to tradition to find different ways to fight against such trends, although such efforts could only be fragile and marginal, or limited to "remote" areas outside the mainstream of modernization.

This argument is valid to some extent. If one examines the works of contemporary Chinese architects, one will find that many of them had a classic modernist phase in their early period of practice, after which they stepped into differentiated design paths and gradually formed an architectural vocabulary with their own characteristics. The most typical example is Wang Shu, the Pritzker Prize laureate, whose early representative works, such as the library of Suzhou University's Wenzheng College, can be attributed to the purist tradition from Le Corbusier to Giuseppe Terragni, but the Xiangshan Campus of the China Academy of Art thereafter is the work that really defines Wang Shu's personal approach. In this sense, the process Frampton describes of embracing modernism first, then moving away from it and attempting to fix the problems it created, is not only reflected in Chinese architectural practice as a whole, but also condensed in the careers of many Chinese architects. This is naturally not an accidental coincidence. It could be attributed in large part to the rapid changes in Chinese society, where the pace of many things, from the economic to the cultural evolution, has accelerated significantly.

However, this narrative of the confrontation between the mainstream and the marginal has its limitations. In order to produce definite generalizations in limited space, the author has to give a simplistic presentation by abandoning complexity to a large extent. Perhaps the most controversial aspect of Frampton's argument is the idea that tradition and modernity confront with each other. In order to map this viewpoint, he has purposely selected some "remote" projects, such as Wang Shu's Wencun Village in Zhejiang Province, the house of Ma Qingyun's father in Nantian, Shaanxi Province, and Niang'ou Pier in Tibet by Zhang Ke. However, the existence of these projects fails to suggest that high-quality contemporary Chinese architecture is primarily located in remote areas, as Beijing, Shanghai, Hangzhou, Chengdu, Qinhuangdao, Jingdezhen, and other major cities and their surroundings are still the most active regions of contemporary Chinese architectural practice. For example, projects such as West Village Yard in Chengdu, designed by Liu Jiakun, and Beijing No. 4 High School Fangshan Campus by OPEN, are situated in China's most advanced metropolises.

Confrontation is one of the most important discourse paradigms in Western architectural theory after World War II. It started with the confrontation of Team 10 against the Athens Charter, and continued with the confrontation of postmodernism against modernism, deconstructionism against traditional rationality, and critical theory against architectural ideology. The critical regionalism advocated by Frampton also unfolds in such confrontational mode, suggesting that it is necessary to "deconstruct" the inherited traditions as well as to maintain a "straightforward critique" of universal culture. However, in China's contemporary cultural context, confrontation is hardly the mainstream mindset as progressive reform has been the dominant paradigm of Chinese society since 1978, which implies continuous experimentation, adaptation, and acceptance. This characteristic is also reflected in architecture, where it is the process of continuous exploration and integration, rather than confrontation and critique, that has driven the development of architectural practice and research the past 40 years. The attraction of confrontation and critique discourse lies in the clear structure of dichotomy with conceptual simplicity and clarity. Progressive innovation, on the other hand, is much more ambiguous and complex, as diverse factors may be involved, not just opposing binaries. But of the two, it is clear that only the latter is more suitable for describing the overall trend of contemporary architecture in China.

This discussion is certainly not meant to criticize Frampton's brief discussion, but rather offers an opportunity to discuss the trending characteristics of contemporary Chinese architecture. For a more comprehensive understanding, it is necessary to be wary of oversimplified generalizations. A relevant example is Frampton's presentation of several works by Dong Gong of Vector Architects, such as Seaside Library in the Beidaihe and Museum of Intangible Heritage in Suzhou, which, according to the author, make use of the mature vocabulary of the European modernist movement and embody typical rationalist qualities. However, what Frampton fails to mention is that during the same period, Dong Gong also completed projects like the Alila Hotel in Yangshuo, Guilin, where he incorporated local elements such as mountain rocks, bamboo rafts, rural houses, and an old sugar factory into the structure. Apparently, it is difficult to categorize such a project into the mature vocabulary of modernism or typical rationalism. As a result, Dong Gong's work cannot be categorized on either side of the confrontation between modernity and tradition, but rather as an integration of the two, as is exemplified by Alila Hotel.

Frampton's thesis that contemporary Chinese architects draw a lot from tradition is very accurate, except that the concept of tradition is extremely broad, and in the absence of a more in-depth analysis, there is a risk of simplifying it as the antithesis of modernity. This is precisely the reason why the text of *Modern Architecture: A Critical History* needs to be scrutinized. To obtain a deeper and more comprehensive understanding, we must analyze the notion of tradition in a more detailed manner and present its relationship with modernity more accurately.

2. Herbalism

In my article "Prometheus and the Herb Collector: A Discussion on the Design of Alila Yangshuo Hotel" published in 2019, I analyzed the different design strategies between the Seaside Library and Alila Yangshuo Hotel. Prometheus in Greek mythology, and the herb collector in the tradition of Chinese medicine, stand as two approaches respectively. Prometheus is a rebel whose independent creation even goes so far as to confront the cosmic order represented by Zeus. This mythical figure symbolizes the free will of the architect as a creator. The herb collector, on the other hand, is an artisan who respects the gifts of the mountains and forests by collecting and processing herbs carefully, and he tries his best to extract the full potential of the herbs as medicine for curing diseases. He symbolizes the humility and dedication of the architect as a collector and craftsman. Taking the image of the herb collector as a blueprint, the current essay suggests that the concept of Herbalism can be used to describe an important trend in contemporary Chinese architectural practice. The purpose of coining this new concept is to provide a more precise and substantial connotation than the broad concept of "tradition," in order to present a more comprehensive picture of the cultural characteristics of many contemporary Chinese architecture.

Herbs, or *Ben Cao* (本草) in the Chinese pinyin system, is a general term for traditional Chinese medicine (TCM), as they are mainly herbaceous. Many traditional Chinese medical books, including *Shennong Ben Cao Jing*, *Tang Ben Cao*, and *Ben Cao Gang Mu*, use the term in this sense. The utilization of this concept in architecture is, of course, a metaphor. But there are different types of metaphors, and one type is the "absolute metaphor" proposed by the German philosopher Hans Blumenberg. He writes: "By providing a point of orientation, the content of absolute metaphors determines a particular attitude or conduct (Verhalten); they give structure to a world, representing the nonexperienceable, nonapprehensible totality of the real." Herbs in this essay is one absolute metaphor in Blumernberg's sense. It is used to indicate a kind of "orientation," a "specific attitude or mode of behavior," so that we change "herbs" to Herbalism to emphasize that it refers to a kind of thinking and philosophical standing. Metaphors can seem vague and imprecise compared to clear logical analysis, but it is this very vagueness and imprecision that enables them to refer to more complex, ambiguous, and grandiose themes by transcending strict logical analysis.

Traditional Chinese medicine, on which Herbalism is based, is itself a core component of Chinese culture, and still plays an important role in people's lives. Traditional Chinese medicine encompasses not only specific medical techniques, but also a philosophical interpretation of the environment, the body, and the change of all things. This essay tries to utilize this philosophical feature of the traditional Chinese medicine system to help define the theoretical tendency of architecture, and at the same time to elucidate the essence of Chinese tradition in a more substantial way.

What is the specific theoretical connotation of the term Herbalism? This paper suggests that the theoretical core of Herbalism can be characterized by four points, namely, "Occasion and Place," "Observing, Listening, Questioning, and Pulse Feeling," "Integration of Body and Spirit," and "Gathering Springs." We will examine them respectively.

The first is "Occasion and Place." The majority of Chinese herbs come from herbaceous and woody plants, whose growing place, as well as the time of year in which they are collected, have a direct impact on their efficacy. Experienced herb collectors need to collect the herbs at the right place and at the right time in the year. Putting an architect in the collector's place, it implies an emphasis on the specific location of a building and its place in local history. Just as a medicinal plant needs to be adapted to its environment and seasonal changes, architecture should also be adapted to its territory, to the local climate, and to the local cultural landscape accumulated over time. A large number of contemporary Chinese architectural works rely on the interpretation of specific "Occasion and Place," such as Wang Shu's Wencun project and Zhang Ke's Niang'ou Pier, which Frampton mentioned, and Dong Gong's Alila Hotel in Yangshuo, which he did not. The concept of "Zai Di," a Chinese word meaning rooted in a place, has been widely used by Chinese architects in recent years. There is considerable overlap between this concept and "Occasion and Place," while the latter emphasizes not only the place, but also the historical background of the place, such as the sugar factory and bamboo rafts in the Alila Hotel.

Next is "Observing, Listening, Questioning, and Pulse Feeling," which is the distinctive diagnostic method of TCM. A doctor comprehensively assesses the patient's state through visual observation, listening to sounds and breath, inquiring about symptoms, and touching the pulse. The crucial aspect here is that besides vision, other perceptions, including hearing and touching, or even direct body interaction are involved in the diagnosis. Transplanting this principle into architecture, "Observing, Listening, Questioning, and Pulse Feeling" refers to the activation of multiple human senses by, and the encouragement of, physical interaction, rather than relying only on visual observation. A phenomenological interpretation of this principle is given by Juhani Pallasmaa in *The Eyes of the Skin*. He emphasizes breaking the dominance of visual images and acknowledges the significant contribution of sound, taste, and touch to architectural experience. In design, these aspects can be strengthened by the special architectural treatment of materials, light, atmosphere, and body movement. One of the most notable trends in contemporary Chinese architecture is the exceptional attention given to materiality. Materials with rich textures, such as raw concrete, rough stones, bricks, wood, and bamboo are widely used by architects in projects in both urban and rural settings. Hua Li's Gaoligong Handmade Paper Museum, Li Ji's Liyang Yangwan Tourist Station, and Zhu Pei's Jingdezhen Imperial Kiln Museum are typical examples of this trend.

The third point is "Integration of Body and Spirit." This term is taken from the ancient medical book *Inner Canon of the Yellow Emperor* (黄帝内经), specifically from the section "Discussion on the Nurture of Life in the Ancient Times." It refers to an ideal state of existence where the body and spirit are in harmonious resonance. According to traditional Chinese medical theory, illness can be caused by both physical and spiritual factors. Therefore, it is important to consider not only the treatment of physical organs but also the adjustment of psychological and spiritual states. In architecture, it implies that as material structures, buildings should also possess spiritual value. However, spiritual value is a very vague concept, and the representation of spiritual value in architecture can be quite challenging. The most common approach is to use meaningful connotations, such as architectural types, symbols, and metaphors. Buildings can convey meanings that evoke profound intellectual resonance, contributing to spiritual value. Architectural interpretations of the "Integration of Body and Spirit Coexisting" principle include Wang Shu's study and representation of Song Dynasty paintings, Li Hu and Huang Wenjing's exploration of the archetypes of caves in the Dune Art Museum, and Zhu Xiaofeng's creation of Jiangnan garden scenes in the Dongyuan Community Center, with its white walls, concave roofs, and water courtyards.

The last point is "Gathering Springs." Both "Gathering" and "Spring" are core concepts in Heidegger's later philosophy. They aim to emphasize that while recognizing the constructive role of human beings in the phenomenal world they inhabit, it is essential to recognize that this construction is not arbitrary but depends on specific springs. Whether they are "things" that cannot be exhausted by any concept, or historical and value concepts that shape our perspectives, they all have their origin in the mysterious springs. Human beings are not creators who create things out of nothing, but collectors and gatherers. It is through the springs that things can be collected, and through gathering and processing, new things can be created, revealing the latent potential of the springs. This is why the author used the concept of "herbalist" earlier. In TCM, the herbalist is such a gatherer, who always maintains reverence for the mountains and forests as he does for the springs, while revealing the medicinal properties inherent in the herbs through his skills. In architecture, therefore, "Gathering Springs" refers more to the attitude and stance of architects than to the characteristics of the architecture itself. As Heidegger said, as gatherers, we should always be humble and maintain humility and respect for the springs, and appreciate the joy of the gifts we receive. An outstanding work of art should reveal the depth of the springs and praise the act of gathering. Architects with such an attitude often demonstrate humility in their works, show respect for the existing traditions of "Time and Place," and use various means such as "Observing, Listening, Questioning, and Pulse Feeling" to bring together multiple architectural values and convey specific meanings. This process enables people to gain a deeper understanding of these values and meanings, which in turn influences their own perceptions and stances, thus achieving—in addition to physical care—the pacification of the spirit—that is, the purpose of "Integration of Body and Spirit." Examples embodying this specific attitude and stance include Li Xiaodong's Bridge Library which gathers the two banks of the stream, Xu Tiantian's honoring of rocks and craftsmanship in the Jinyun Quarry, and Liu Yichun's interpretation of the long wall in the Bian Yuan.

2.1 Herbalism and Traditional Philosophy

Although it may seem unusual to mention Heidegger in the context of "Herbalism," it becomes more understandable when taking into account Heidegger's deep engagement with the ancient Chinese book *Tao Te Ching* (道德经) in his later writings. According to British philosopher David Cooper's interpretation, Heidegger was interested in the concept of "Spring" in ancient Chinese philosophy. The spring precedes any language, concept, or thought, and cannot be accurately described. Therefore, it can be referred to as "Tao" or even "emptiness." The crucial point is to reveal the depth of the Spring, and to understand that we are also parts of the Spring, rather than isolated entities with unconstrained, and independent free will. In an interesting paper titled "Jewish and Christian Elements in Philosophy: Their Share in the Emergence of the Modern Mind," German philosopher Hans Jonas traces the idea of the dualistic opposition between spiritual consciousness and the material world in modern Western thought back to the notion in both the Jewish and Christian religion that God created everything out of nothing. According to his reasoning, God relies on nothing and is independent of everything He creates. Over time, humans have gradually assumed the role of the God, evolving into a spiritual will different and separated from everything else in the world. According to Jonas, existentialism epitomizes this dualism to its extreme, leading to the isolation and nihilism of human existence. Therefore, it is not difficult then to understand that Heidegger's emphasis on the Spring is one way to counter this dualism. Furthermore, he believed that only by acknowledging the Spring can individuals find a truly dependable foundation for values, thus remedying the crisis of modernity.

If we accept Heidegger's discussions, Herbalism or "Herbal Architecture," which share similar philosophical principles, may emerge as a therapeutic method in contemporary society. Beyond offering utility, architecture can shape perspectives and focus through meaning and revelation, impacting individuals' perceptions and understandings, thus contributing to addressing underlying intellectual issues. To borrow Blumenberg's discourse again, "Herbal Architecture" is an absolute metaphor for contemporary culture, pointing toward a particular attitude, behavior, and understanding of the world and ourselves. This bears a striking resemblance to the role that traditional Chinese medicine plays in contemporary society. An outstanding traditional Chinese medicine doctor not only prescribes herbal remedies but also offers advice on the patient's lifestyle and even psychological well-being. As a rich component of Chinese traditional culture, traditional Chinese medicine emphasizes the holistic integration of humans with the sky, earth, time, and people. An ideal state of health is achieved by finding a harmonious state that aligns with the overall natural trend rather than through the isolated treatment of the physical body. This requires a correct understanding of individuals within the larger context, and adjusting their lifestyle accordingly to serve the overall well-being of individuals as a whole. This aligns with the responsibilities bestowed upon architecture by modern architectural pioneers such as Frank Lloyd Wright and Sigfried Giedion.

The concept of Herbalism is deeply rooted in the rich heritage of Chinese traditional medicine spanning thousands of years. This tradition remains vibrant today and exerts a profound influence on people's daily lives. The continuity of this tradition, combined with the openness to and assimilation of external influences, is a defining feature of Chinese culture, making it exceptionally enduring among ancient civilizations. It is in this context that we called for the further refinement of Frampton's narrative of modernity versus tradition within contemporary Chinese architectural practice. While an exclusive focus on architectural vocabulary reveals stark differences between modern and traditional Chinese architecture, a deeper exploration into the intellectual foundation of Chinese society suggests that this dualistic narrative may overlook the persistent existence of traditional wisdom and underestimate its contemporary relevance.

Just as traditional Chinese medicine remains an effective means of medical treatment in the digital age, Herbalism has the potential to provide remedies for architecture and society. Following Heidegger's later discourse, Herbalism aims to restore not merely the damage caused by rapid urbanization, but also the existential problems brought about by modernity as a whole. Similar to the Black Forest farmstead, a house Heidegger mentioned in his famous essay "Building Dwelling Thinking," which imparts insights into the holistic existence of human beings, the exemplary Herbalism architecture discussed earlier can offer guidance on people's contemporary way of life. This architectural philosophy can benefit anyone who understands and accepts it, not just the Chinese.

It is essential to emphasize that Herbalism refers more to design strategies rather than to a specific design vocabulary. Whether it is Wang Shu's "Wapan" (瓦爿), Dong Gong's plain concrete, or Zhu Xiaofeng's steel-wood structures, all can be considered to be in line with the Herbalism tendency. The construction of a thought system above a metaphysical foundation is an essential characteristic of traditional Chinese civilization, exemplified by Confucianism's "*Ren*" and "*Li*," Daoist philosophy's "*Dao*," and the yin-yang concept in traditional Chinese medicine. Likewise, Herbalism underscores this foundational aspect. Whether it is the place, the historical background, the climatic characteristics, or the materials and structures on which the building is based, the architect can choose his or her own place of interest to focus on. But in any case, a "Herbalist" architect understands that architectural design does not come out of thin air, but relies on some kind profound Springs, and the more the quality and potential of these Springs can be explored, the higher the humanistic value it will have. In fact, similar qualities can be seen not only in Chinese architects, but also in Western architects such as Alvaro Siza, Peter Zumthor, and Glenn Murcutt.

One simple fact is that the use of herbal medicine is not exclusive to the Chinese. In ancient Greece and Rome, herbal medicine was also widely employed. Today, herbal plants continue to play various roles globally, not just as medicinal remedies but also as food flavorings. Therefore, Herbalism might resonate in these places as well. We also hope that as an architectural idea, Herbalism has the potential to transcend geographical boundaries and provide new insights for the exploration of contemporary architectural theories around the world.

Notes

1. Kenneth Frampton, *Modern Architecture: A Critical History*, fifth edition (London, United Kingdom: 2020), 492.
2. Kenneth Frampton, "Towards a Critical Regionalism: Six Points for an Architecture of Resistance," in *Postmodern Culture*, ed. Hal Foster (United Kingdom: London: Bay Press, 1983), 21.
3. Frampton, *Modern Architecture: A Critical History*, 496.
4. See Qing Feng, "Prometheus and the Herb Collector: A Discussion on the Design of the Alila Yangshuo Hotel," *Times + Architecture*, no. 1 (2019).
5. Hans Blumenberg and Robert Savage, *Paradigms for a Metaphorology, Signale : Modern German Letters, Cultures, and Thought* (Ithaca, N.Y.: Cornell University Press: Cornell University Library, 2010), 14.
6. See Juhani Pallasmaa, *The Eyes of the Skin: Architecture and the Senses*, third edition (Chichester, United Kingdom: Wiley, 2012), Part 2.
7. See Martin Heidegger, "Building Dwelling Thinking," in *Basic Writings*, ed. David Farrell Krell (San Francisco, United States: Harper Collins, 1993).
8. David E. Cooper, *The Measure of Things: Humanism, Humility, and Mystery* (Oxford, United Kingdom: Oxford University Press, 2002), 334.
9. Hans Jonas, "Jewish and Christian Elements in Philosophy: Their Share in the Emergence of the Modern Mind," in *Philosophical Essays: From Ancient Creed to Technological Man*, ed. Hans Jonas (Englewood Cliffs, N.J.: Prentice-Hall, 1974).

Four Studio-Houses

Bird's-eye view of the four studio-houses and the Education Forum at Dongqian Lake

Architect firm: Atelier FCJZ
Principal architect: Yung Ho Chang, Lijia Lu
Design team: Liang Xiaoning, Huang Shuyi, Wu Zhuqing, Han Shukai, Zhang Min, He Zelin
Location: Ningbo, Zhejiang Province, China
Area: 3,900 square meters
Completion date: 2022
Photography: Tian Fangfang, Li Keliang

An Education and Art Community

The Education Forum at Dongqian Lake in Ningbo, Zhejiang Province, China is a community that includes a convention center, a hotel, an art museum, villas, and other facilities. The owner is passionate about education as well as art and in line with that, a group of four studio-houses have been built specifically to accommodate visitors, especially scholars or artists who may come for an extended visit to either conduct research and/or work on creative projects.

Design as Research

Three of the four studio-houses were conceived by Yung Ho Chang without client nor site in the early 1990s as an attempt to blur the line between classicism and modernism. These "paper architecture" are dual-purposed: as serious investigations on a core issue of architecture—space—and as buildable propositions. This particular aspect of the project and its history make these four pieces of architecture apt inclusions in the discussion and exchange of ideas on art and research at the Forum.

Prototyping Space

The studio-houses are meant as experiments to test out ways to organize architectural spaces. The openness of the work-live program creates the leeway to structure four distinctly different spatial conditions. Designing a space can never be separate from imagining the experience as well as lifestyle within it. Each of the four studio-houses is respectively named after an architectural element that characterizes each of their spatial organization. They are: House with Face-to-Face Loggias, House with Cruciform Glass, House with Walkable Beam, and House with Flipped Roof.

House with Face-to-Face Loggias

A symmetrical volume has been imagined as being sliced in the middle and pulled apart to accommodate a pool flanked by two loggias on the ground level, one on each side. The two facing loggias define the open space in-between, framing both outdoor and semi-outdoor events.

The inhabitant needs to cross the water court from the living quarters to work in the study on the other side, and then cross it again on the way back, which creates a transition ritual of daily living. Sitting in a loggia and talking to a friend is another pleasure the house offers. And at that moment, the relationship of the loggias morphs into that of people.

House with Cruciform Glass

On the ground level, spaces are organized with a pinwheel formation; on the upper level, a transparent volume is divided into four equal quarters for living, cooking/dining, sleeping, and bathing by a hollow cruciform double curtain wall that connects the second floor to the ground below.

The space in the upper floor glass house is simultaneously opened and divided. The inhabitant may move along the outer glass curtain wall, enjoying a panoramic view of the surrounding water court, which is punctured by sceneries that filter in through the cuts in the peripheral wall.

House with Walkable Beam

A double-height space for a plastic art studio is bookended with two oversized porches and floats in the middle of a walkable cruciform beam.

The inhabitant's creative process unfolds around the beam: standing on it to examine his/her art on the walls or hanging beneath it as work-in-progress pieces; or crossing it on his/her way to the library.

House with Flipped Roof

A single space is divided by an inverted sloped roof into two zones: one for work and one for living.

This inhabitant lives and works almost in the same space. Visually, live and work areas on opposite sides of the inverted roof have limited connection, yet whichever side the inhabitant is in, he/she would be constantly aware of the other. This studio-house juxtaposes combination and separation.

Materiality

Reinforced concrete is used like clay to mold pure spaces in these four studio-houses. The textured surface of the exposed concrete, created by being poured in timber formwork is intended to avoid abstraction and give an expression of tangibility to the spaces.

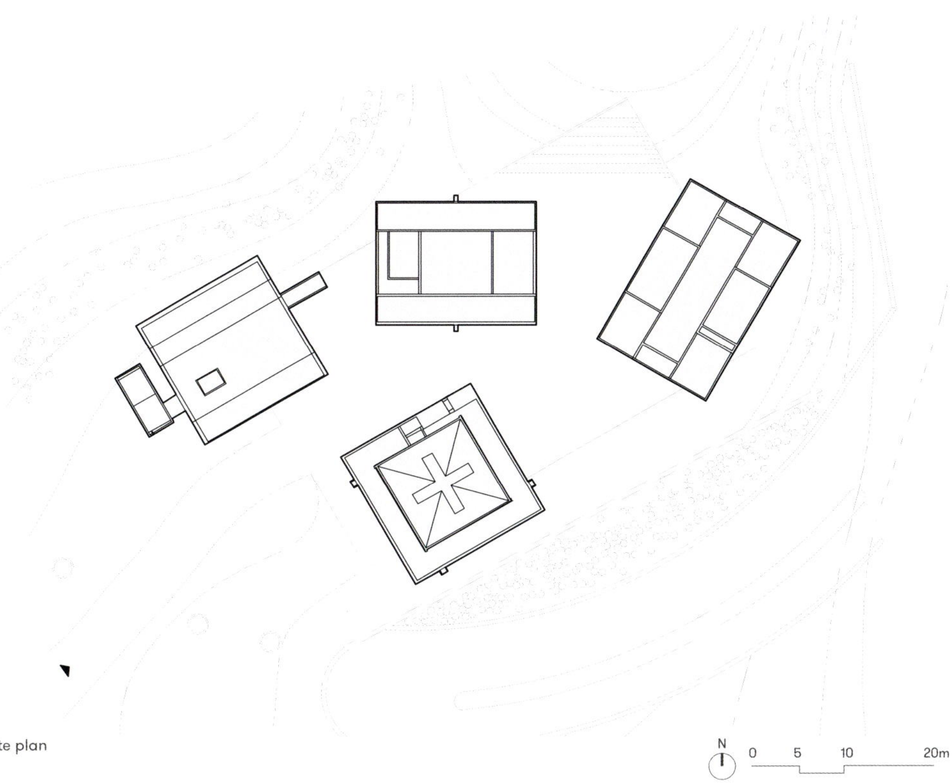

Site plan

House with Face-to-Face Loggias: Water-court between the living quarters and the study quarters

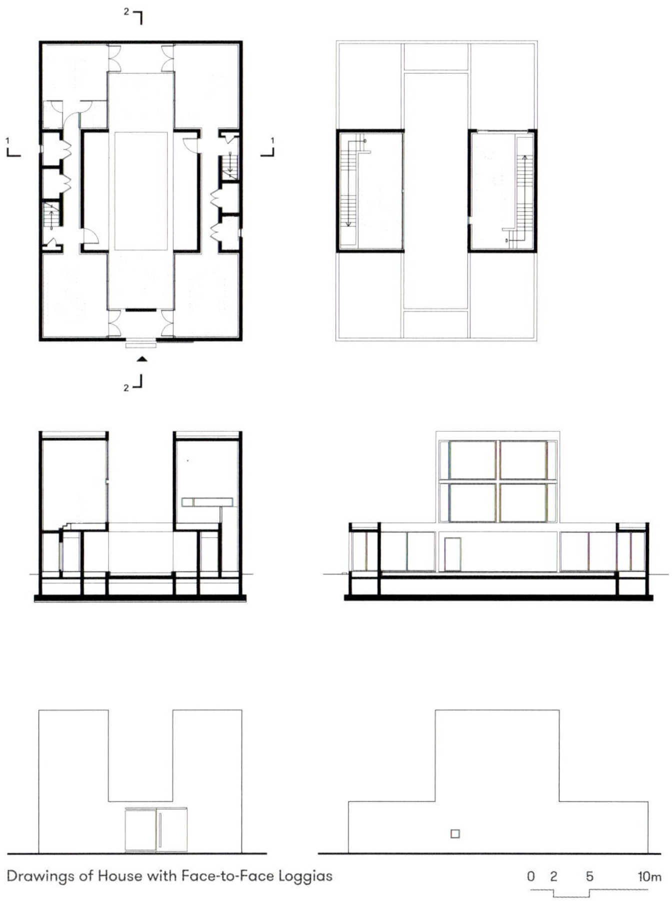

Drawings of House with Face-to-Face Loggias

House with Cruciform Glass: Cruciform semi-outdoor space on the first floor

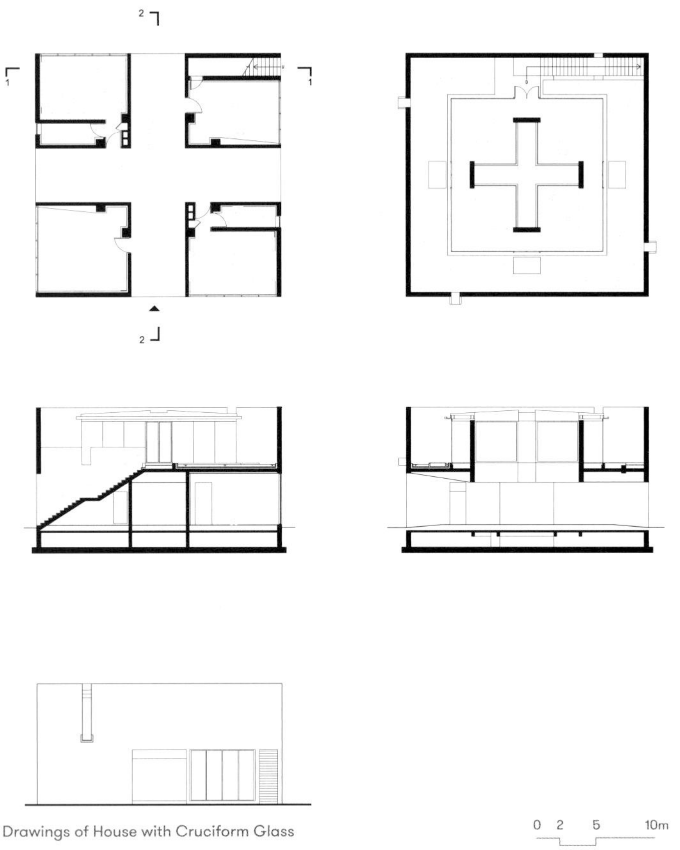

Drawings of House with Cruciform Glass

House with Cruciform Glass: Four rooms on the second floor divided by cruciform hollow glass curtain walls

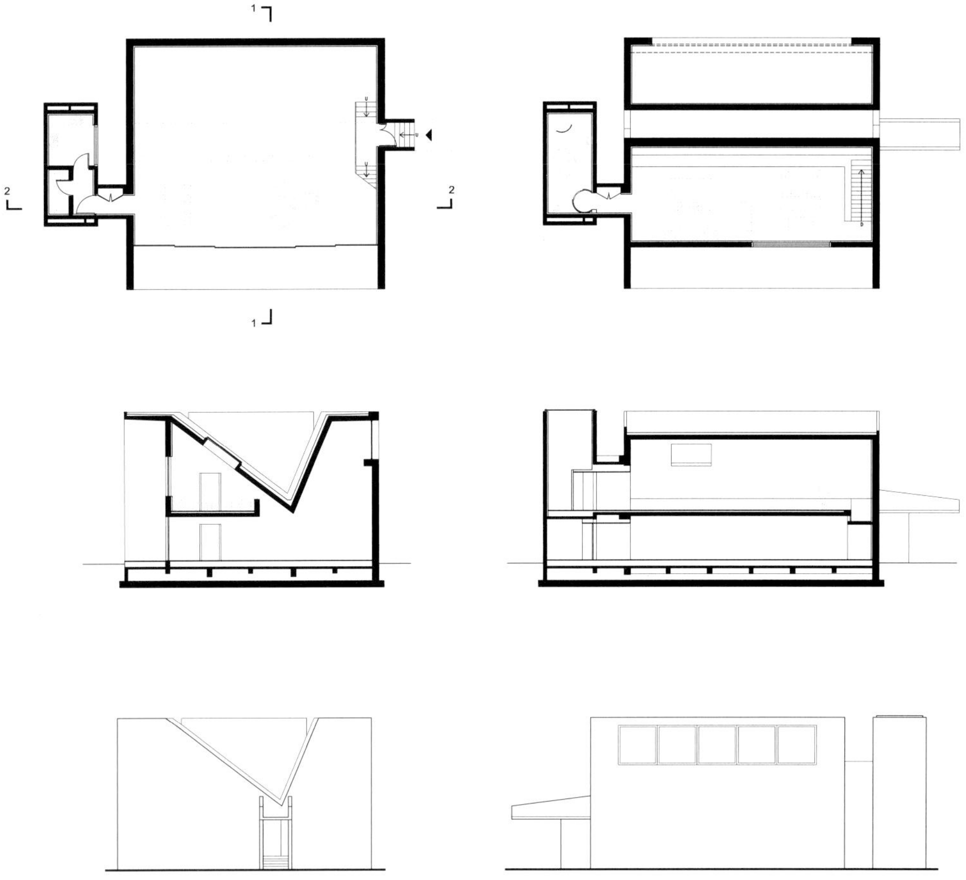

Drawings of House with Flipped Roof

House with Flipped Roof

House with Walkable Beam on the left

House with Walkable Beam: View from the walkable cruciform beam

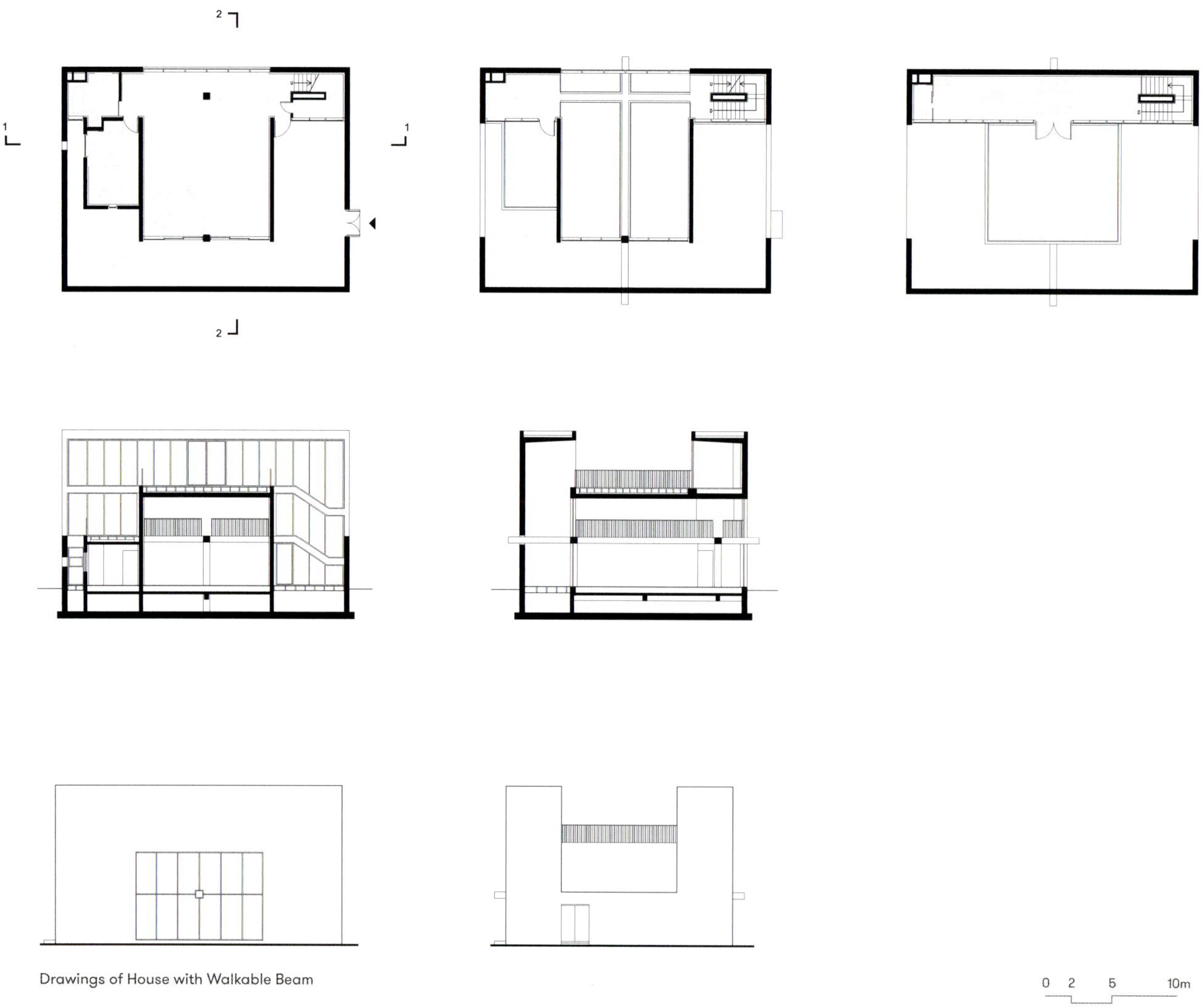
Drawings of House with Walkable Beam

House with Walkable Beam: Beam running through the building and courtyard

National Sliding Center ("Snow Flying Dragon")

Winding "Snow Flying Dragon"

Architect firm: China Architecture Design & Research Group
Principal architect: Li Xinggang
Design team: Li Xinggang, Qiu Jianbing, Zhang Yuting, Liu Ziqi, Zhu Lingli, Yuan Zhimin
Location: Beijing, China
Area: 52,500 square meters
Completion date: September 2020
Photography: Sun Haiting

National Sliding Center (Snow Flying Dragon) is located on a narrow south-facing ridge in the valley at the southern foothills of Yanqing Xiaohaituo Mountain, Beijing, China, covering an area of 9.5 hectares with a building area of 52,500 square meters. It hosted the 2022 Beijing Winter Olympic's bobsleigh, skeleton, and luge events. The venue is built against the mountain, with a north–south span of 800 meters and a maximum east–west width of 300 meters. The venue has an elevation difference of 141 meters, with an average slope of 16 percent. The track is 1,975 meters long with a vertical drop of 121 meters, and features sixteen different curves with varying angles and slopes, including Curve 11, which is a spectacular over 360 degrees spiral turn, resembling a dragon spiraling through the mountain valley.

As China's first sliding venue, "Snow Flying Dragon" was designed along the core concept of "Mountain Forest Venue and Ecological Winter Olympics," around the Yanqing competition zone. The design comprehensively considered the challenges brought by the mountain and forest environment to venue planning and construction, aiming to create a Winter Olympics venue where architectural landscapes and the natural environment would seamlessly merge, thereby meeting the requirements of the exciting sports events that would be hosted, while establishing a harmonious coexistence between each specific sport and the ecological mountain and forest environment.

To address issues caused by climate conditions, such as sunlight radiation on the south-facing slopes, the design team developed the track "Terrain Weather Protection System." This system, in combination with natural and artificial topography and shading canopies, provides all-around, all-time protection for the track surface. Additionally, a parallel roof viewing walkway system was also designed above the entire track to accommodate spectators, allowing "Snow Flying Dragon" to both echo the geographical scale of the landscape with its nearly 2-kilometer architectural length, as well as cater to people engaging in sports or a leisurely stroll.

Due to the narrow and compact mountainous terrain on which the track and venue were constructed, the design team independently developed the complex terrain outdoor venue and the building BIM integration design technology. This ensured the effective implementation of track weather protection strategies and precise control of venue and building models in different functional zones. It allowed for the efficient organization of the track and various functional areas that were subjected to the complex mountain conditions, as well as a high degree of alignment between the venue and the site. The design and construction of "Snow Flying Dragon" made extensive use of natural materials such as roof wooden tiles and stone gabion curtain walls that were constructed using crushed stones from the site.

As a professional venue for bobsleigh competitions, "Snow Flying Dragon" was opened to the public as an Olympic legacy after the Games. It's available for visitors to experience the track by riding specialized sleds from a public starting point, or explore the entire venue on foot via the roof walkway while enjoying the surrounding forested environment.

The nearby Xidazhuangke Village, which underwent a comprehensive transformation, retains its original village layout, while adding ice and snow service industry facilities to support post-Olympic public snowfield operations. Village residents have been resettled and have become part of the public ice and snow industry workforce, changing the traditional ways of life and production in the village. The symbiotic and shared relationship between "Snow Flying Dragon" and the surrounding facilities will bring long-term sustainable development to the Yanqing region.

"Snow Flying Dragon" site plan

The body scale of the "Snow Flying Dragon"

Overall aerial view of Yanqing competition zone

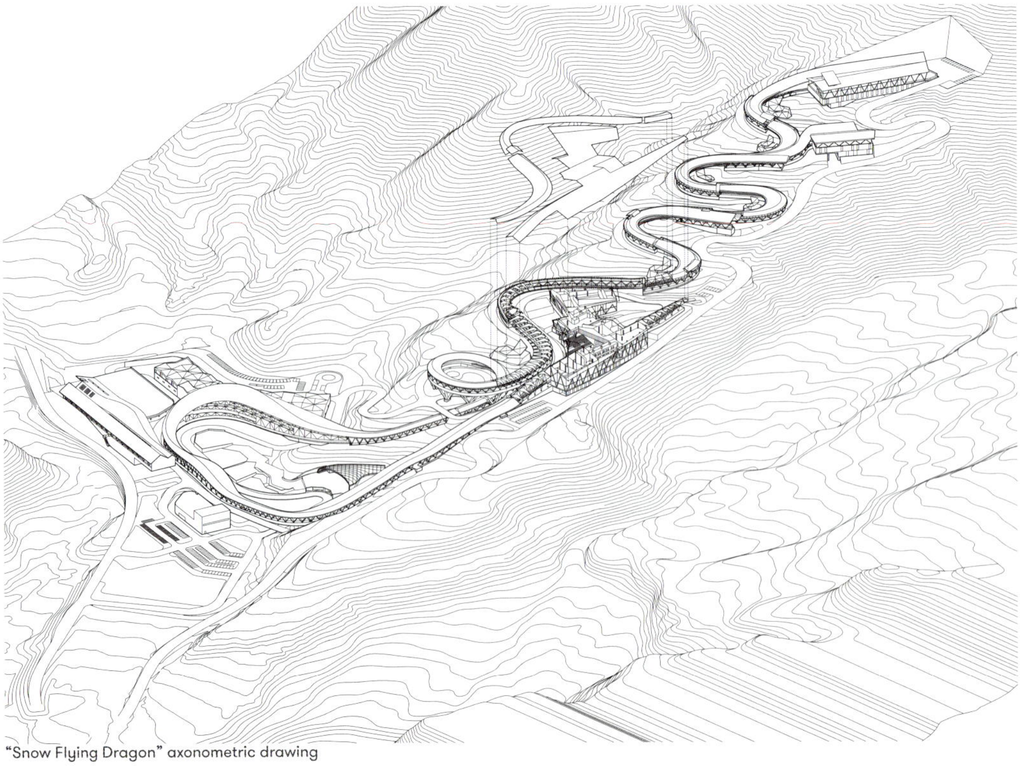
"Snow Flying Dragon" axonometric drawing

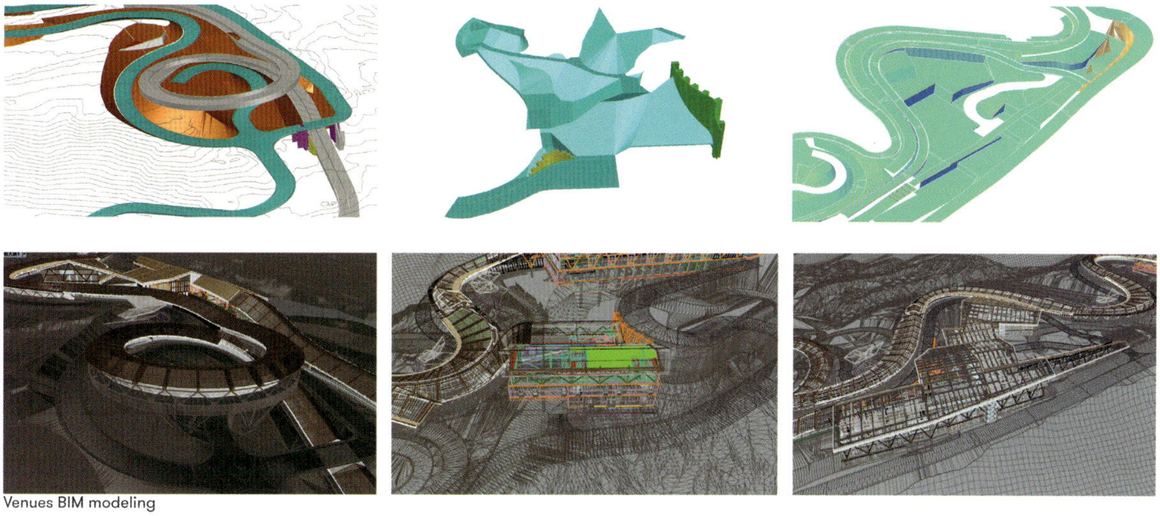
Venues BIM modeling

The geographic scale of the "Snow Flying Dragon"

The body scale of the "Snow Flying Dragon"—sports competition

View of Xidazhuangke Village from the "Snow Flying Dragon"

Track "Terrain Weather Protection System"

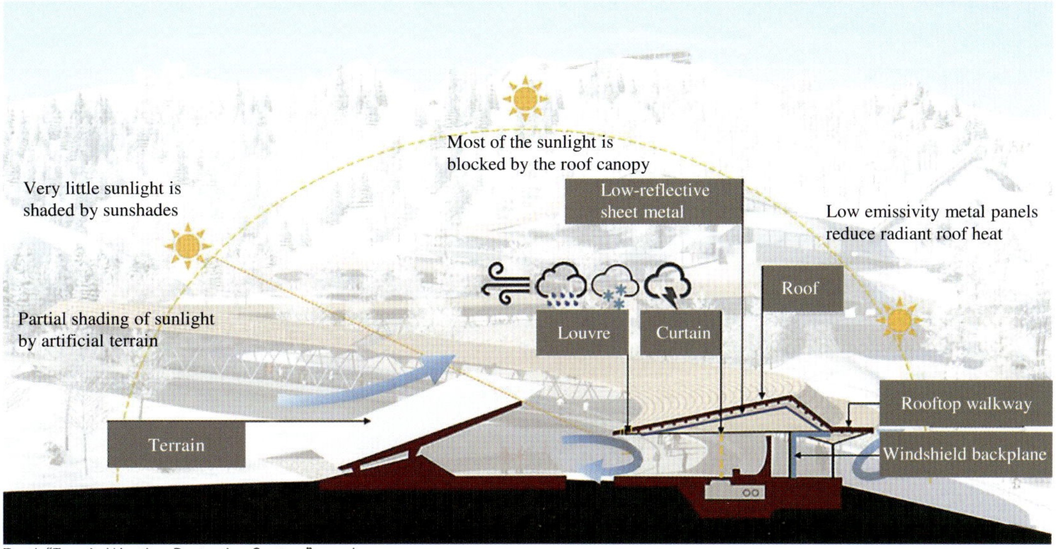

Track "Terrain Weather Protection System" graph

Rooftop walkway

View of Start House 2 from the rooftop walkway

Rooftop walkway and surrounding mountain environment

Kingway Brewery Renovation

Partial aerial view

Architect firm: URBANUS
Principal architect: Yan Meng
Building renovation:
Project manager: (Design development) Haijun Zhang; (bidding) Wendy Wu
Project architect: (Design development) Ting Wen; (bidding) Milutin Cerovic
Team: (Design development) Ruoning Ni, Zhidi Cheng, Ruizhe Yuan, Wenhan Dong, Ran Yue, Yanyu Lin, Guotong Liao; (bidding) Zhi Zheng, Ran Yue; (internship) Rui Li, Rachael H. Gaydos, Jingxian Huang, Yuchu Wang, Kan Lin, Qingyue Gao, Yining Chen, Chengjie Zhang, Jie Zhou
Landscape design:
Project architect: Xuejuan Zhang
Project manager: Guanda Li
Team: Jiangchen Zhu, Yufeng Gao
Research and curation:
(Director) Wendy Wu; (execution) Siying Wu, Yuxin Liu; (exhibition research) Ruixin Yang, Qinxue Wang; (bidding development) Qinxue Wang; (bidding) Sifei Mo, Hongrui Zhu; (internship) Yu Song, Yuanlu Peng
Location: Shenzhen, China
Area: 12,309 square meters
Completion date: 2022
Photography: Right Angle Image, TAL

Located in downtown Shenzhen City, the Kingway Brewery has been mostly demolished, leaving scattered industrial remnants across 11,600 square meters. Through innovative design strategies of integration, insertion, and intervention, the industrial buildings and equipment remnants have been creatively transformed into urban public spaces encompassing exhibition venues, performance areas, restaurants, bars, shops and landscaped gardens. As the main venue of the 2022 Shenzhen-Hongkong Bi-City Biennale of Urbanism\Architecture, it also served as WORK Number 0 for the exhibition.

The building type of Kingway Brewery provides a unique spatial experience with free-standing structures that are scattered loosely. The design connects several industrial buildings by scooping out volumes of the existing plinth, form intervention, and integration. The plinth is a legacy landform barricading the brewery, which measured 1.65 meters above the street on the westbound, and 3 meters on the east. Now permeable for paths coalescing the scattered structures to confront the new urban complex, it has been transformed into a porous terrain. Visitors are encouraged to meander through the industrial past to the present cityscape alongside the themed gardens and the various openings.

The main approach for the renovation was to preserve the existing concrete buildings and implement nodal spatial interventions. Each building was assessed for its appearance, structure, and load-bearing capacity, and individualized renovations and reinforcement were carried out to create flexible activity spaces. It was akin to an archaeological excavation—uncovering the industrial architectural remnants buried underground and stripping away the covering layers to showcase the original texture of concrete. Handmade ceramic tiles, precast concrete panels with glass aggregates, and terrazzo flooring have been utilized, along with materials like foam aluminum and cast aluminum, to create a contrasting texture with the rough and solid quality of concrete.

During the redesign of the Kingway Brewery, extensive research and exhibition planning were conducted for its future operations. The design concept implemented the plan of "space as exhibition," starting from the exploration and transformation of the site's value. Through flexible spatial interventions and the creative use of industrial equipment remnants, the design aimed to transcend ordinary spatial experiences. By intervening the temporal and spatial sequence of the original industrial production line, diverse spaces have been generated for exhibitions, performances, and activities, resulting in a series of unique spatial experiences.

The spatial layout of the industrial remnants within the site has been preserved in its entirety. Within the plinth, a series of sunken courtyards, passageways, and activity spaces have been excavated from north to south of the existing underground areas. The original buildings serve as the foundation, with steel structure boxes that have been added on top as exhibition halls or to house art installations. Key locations have been chosen to introduce new circulation paths to create interesting and uniquely functional layouts at a low cost. Visitors can enter the dissected original sewage stations, walk through corridors formed by beer fermentation tanks of various sizes and pipelines, as well as explore the underground excavated settling tanks and experience a series of spatial encounters beyond everyday industrial architecture and their equipment.

The plinth incorporates six evacuation staircases located in a row on its western side; this becomes the entrance connecting to the commercial plaza. On the eastern side of the plinth, the enclosed façade opens multiple entrances, activating the 266-meter-long street. Additionally, small squares are set up at the northern and southern ends of the site, fully activating the boundaries of the entire plot in all four directions. This successful transformation not only preserves the area's urban memory but also turns the city block from a single-production factory area into a vibrant cultural and artistic landmark where diverse lifestyles converge.

Partial aerial view

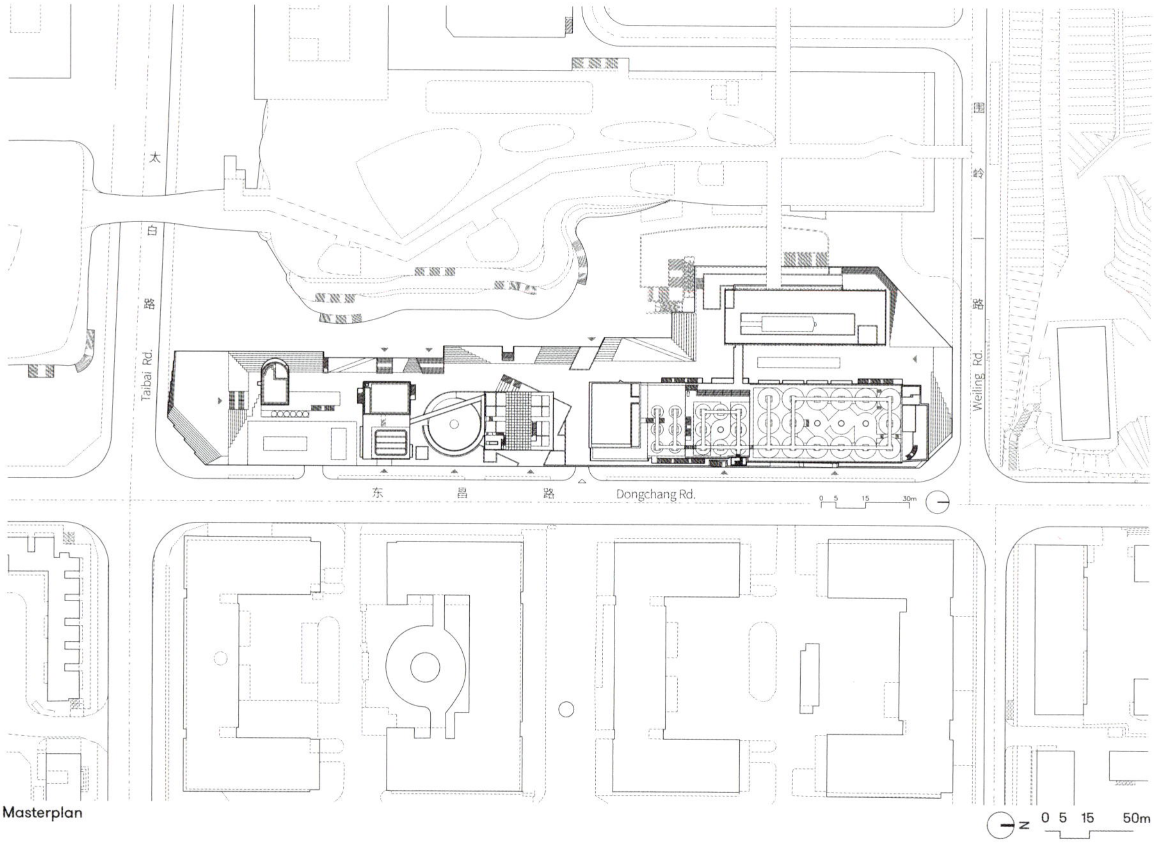

Masterplan

0 5 15 50m

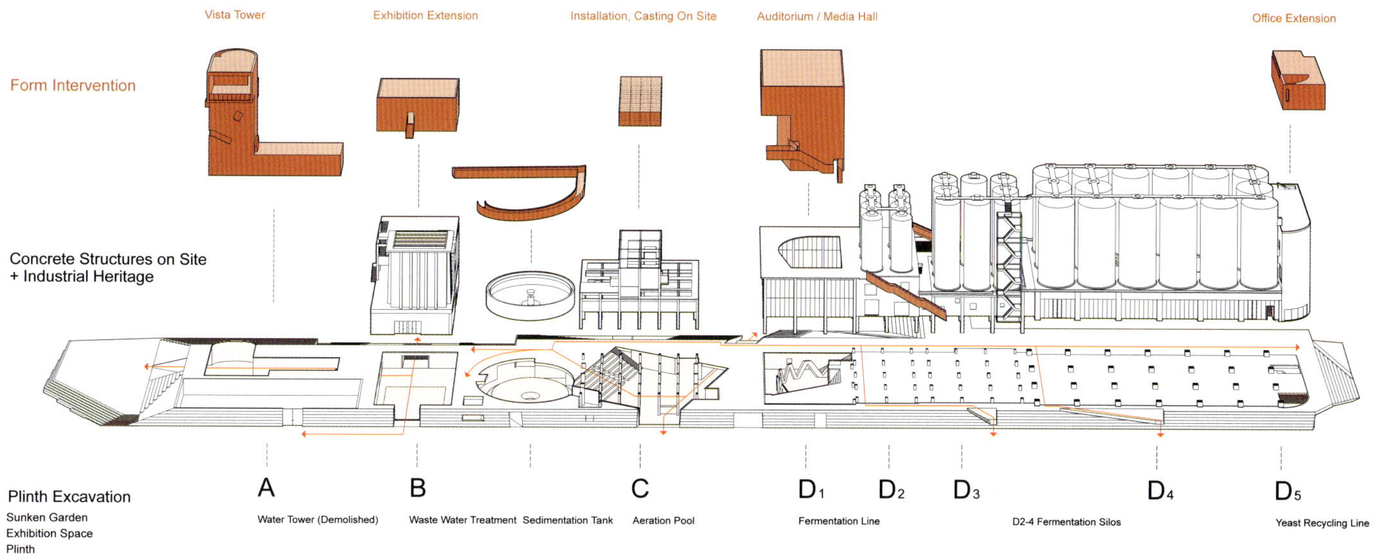

Renovation strategies

Partial aerial view

North elevation of vista tower

Interior of vista tower

View from vista tower

Installation, "Casting On Site"

Inside "Casting On Site"

Interior of B tower

Sedimentation tank after renovation

Sunken courtyard of C tower

Silo theater

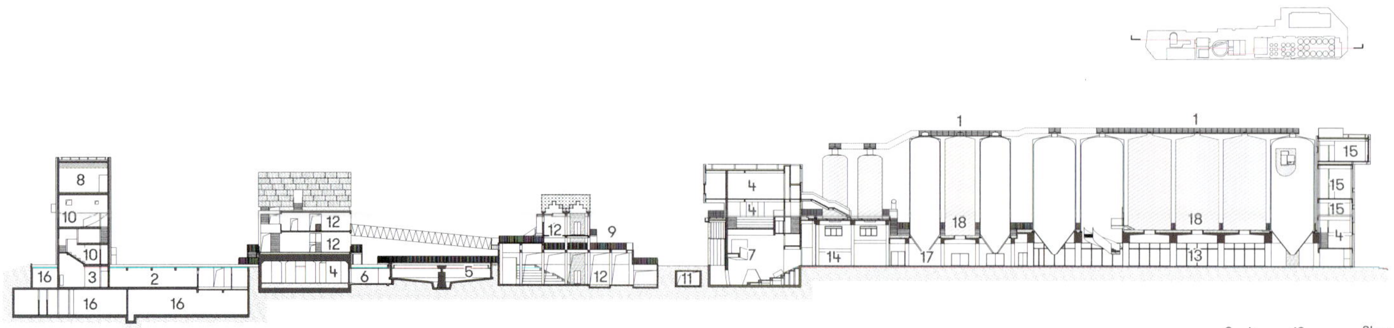

Section

1. Maintenance access
2. Reception/info center
3. Lobby
4. Gallery
5. Water feature
6. Aisle
7. Exhibition/multifunctional hall
8. Viewing platform
9. Aerial walkway
10. Sightseeing (circulation) space
11. Parking entrance
12. Exhibition/Remains of wastewater treatment infrastructure
13. Silo exhibition space
14. Permanent exhibition
15. Administration office
16. Mechanical room
17. Beer-tasting
18. Silo roof

Partial elevation on Dongchang Road

Northeast view of D5 tower

RuiXue Multi-hall, Chengdu

Perspective view of the project

Architect firm: College of Architecture and Urban Planning, Tongji University
Principal architect: Philip F. Yuan
Design team: Weizhe Gao, Xiangping Kong, Bei Zhang, Ju Wang, Yingzi Hu
Location: Sichuan Province, China
Area: 2,180 square meters
Completion date: 2022
Photography: Schran Images, Arch-Exist, Wongke

RuiXue Multi-hall is located in Tianfu Agricultural Expo Park in Xinjin District, Chengdu City, Sichuan Province, surrounded by large fields. The project attempts to integrate the spirit of place with new concepts in future architecture and new technologies under the guidance of structural performance design and the digital construction technology of building robotics.

The design began by tackling the linear boundary conditions of the site, manipulating the strict land-use restrictions to create a free and continuous space that flows deliberately. An undulating terrain embodies the form of the space and showcases engaging sceneries that display a sense of spatial vitality and visual expression, like the earth covered in white snow during winter. Based on this, the design presents the scene of snow-covered landscapes with a white free-form roof, artistically interpreting the beauty of snow falling on the ground. At the same time, it blends with the surrounding natural scenery and cultural spirit, exhibiting the silent integration and mutual complementation between design and environment.

The free-form nature of the shell surface and the connectivity of the internal space guided the design to embody the concept of form through a column-free space, and combined with locally available wood, a reciprocal structure formed by wooden poles was chosen as the overall structural system. The reciprocal structure is a type of reciprocal geometry formed by the lap of bar units, and its units form a grid structure in space where the bars receive each other and transfer loads. In the unwavering commitment to environmental sustainability, the design team selected spruce plywood, known for its eco-friendly attributes, and utilized low-carbon processing methods. Leveraging on a meticulous design and rigorous calculations, they seamlessly integrated the reciprocal timber frame design concept with cutting-edge intelligent construction technology. This synthesis ensured both a robust structural performance, as well as practical construction feasibility. The project offers fresh perspectives and paves the way for innovative wood structure designs within the realm of intelligent construction.

The roof adopts a hyperbolic geometry with complex curvature changes, which imposes high requirements on the efficiency of the structure and the use of materials. A highly optimized structural positioning method known as "reciprocal timber structure system" was employed. By overlapping hexagonal unit wooden beams, an interlocking load-bearing system was formed, achieving optimal structural efficiency and material usage. This method balances the strength and stability of the structure while utilizing the properties of the materials more effectively. Computational design and CNC technology have fundamentally changed material composition and the design concepts of architecture to achieve the best overall coordination between design and structure.

As we transition into an era where rural architectural practices are being revisited and redefined, the RuiXue Multi-hall project, anchored in the ethos of rural revitalization, stands as a testament to what is achievable. This project is not just a building; it is a living manifesto that challenges, reinterprets, and sets new benchmarks across design paradigms, construction techniques, and operational sustainability. By championing novel structural optimization methods, advancing prefabricated assembly techniques, and committing to green ecological resilience, this landmark serves as a touchstone, catalyzing a paradigm shift in rural architectural practices in China, setting the stage for future innovations.

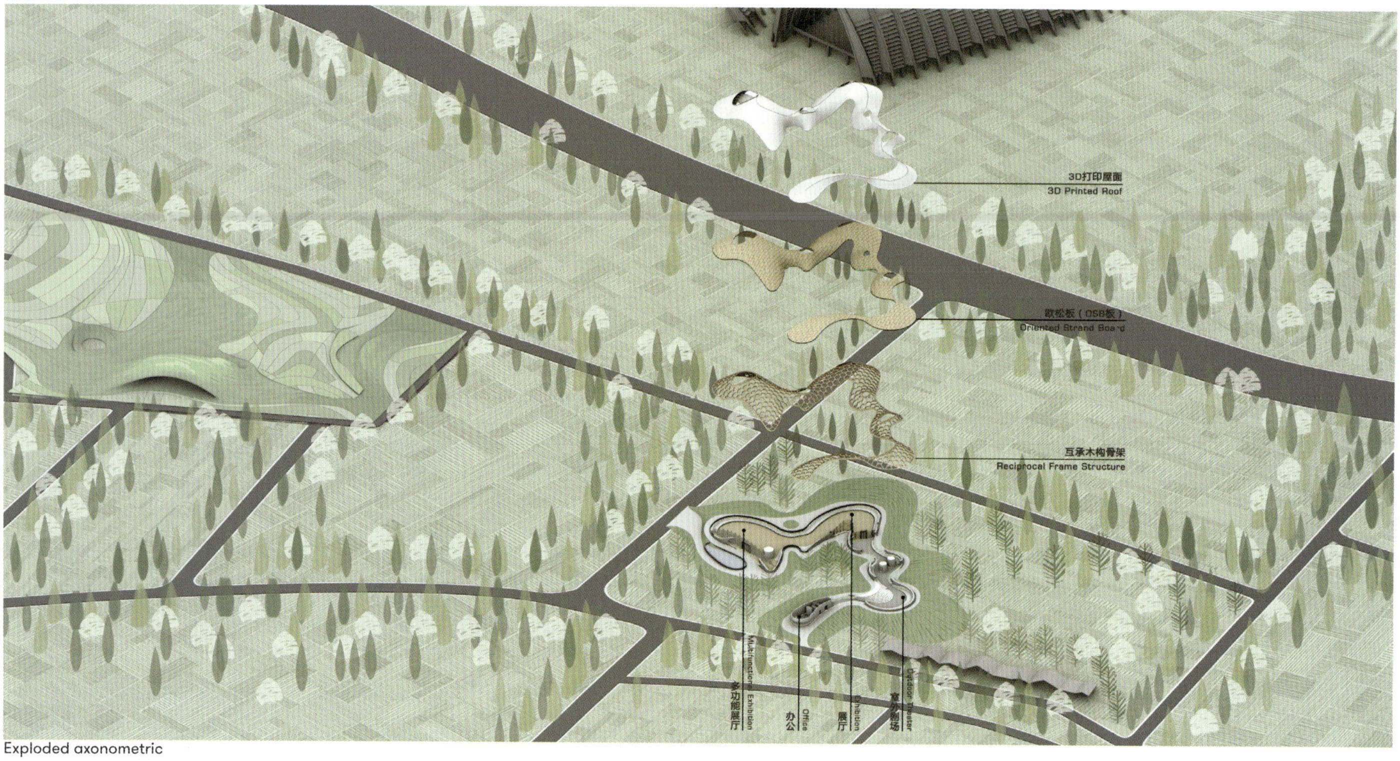

Exploded axonometric

Top view of the roof

Site plan

Aerial view of the project

Perspective view of the project

Perspective view of the project

Perspective view of the project

Perspective of the project

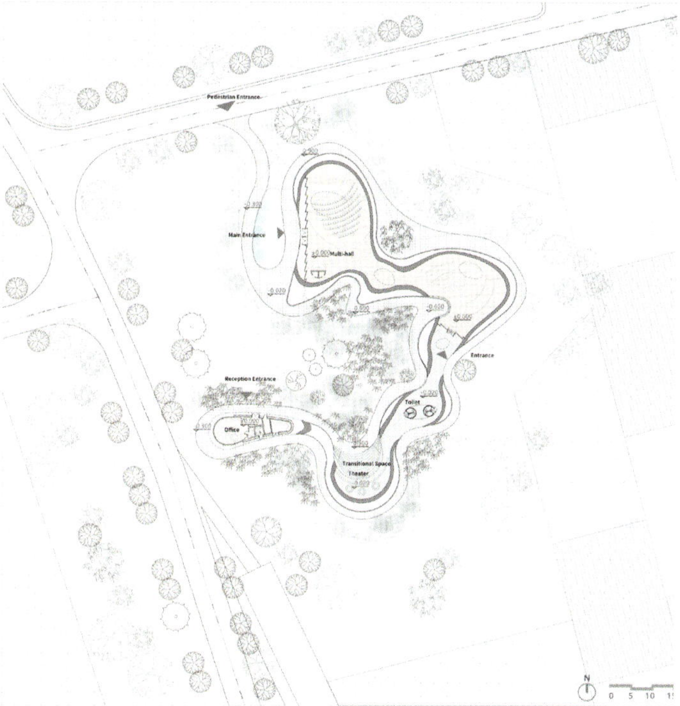

Ground-floor plan

Roof detail

Transition between interior and exterior space

Interior space

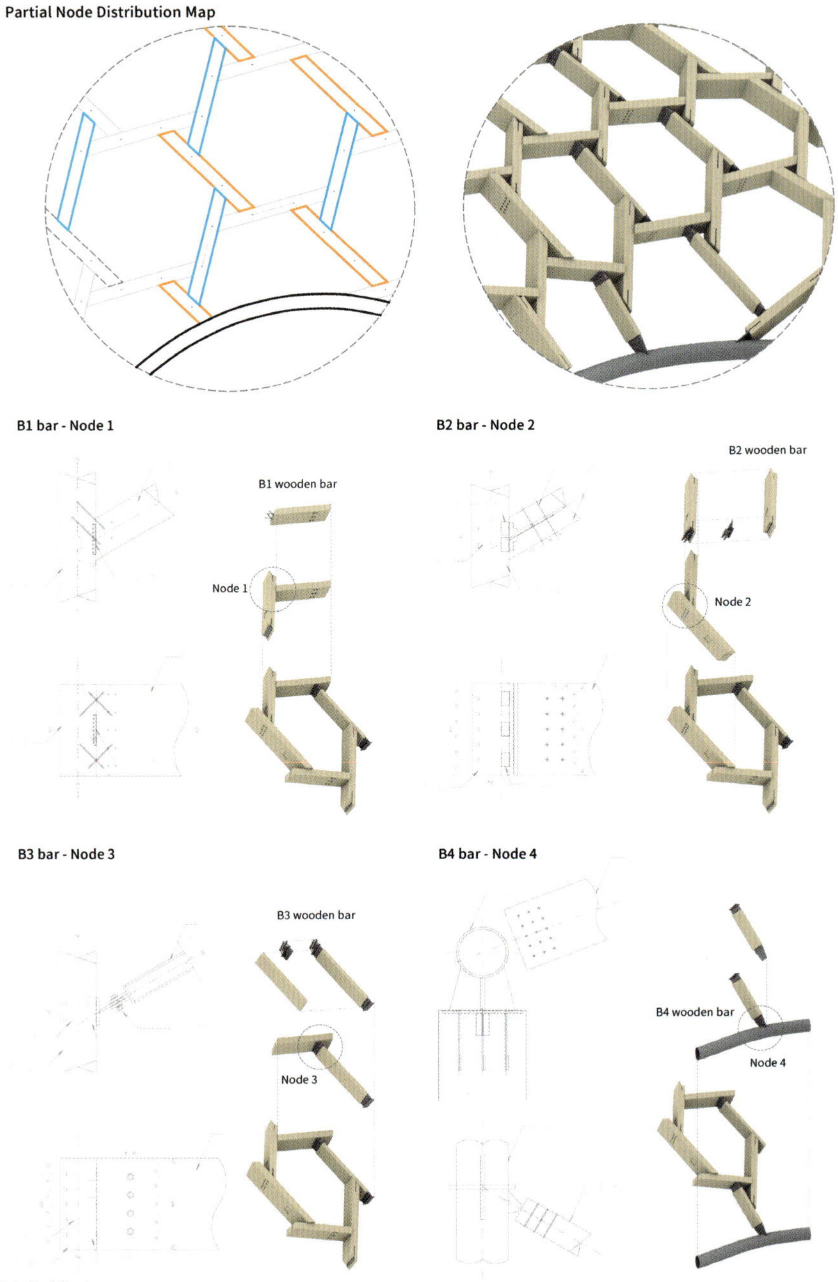

Detail of Nodes

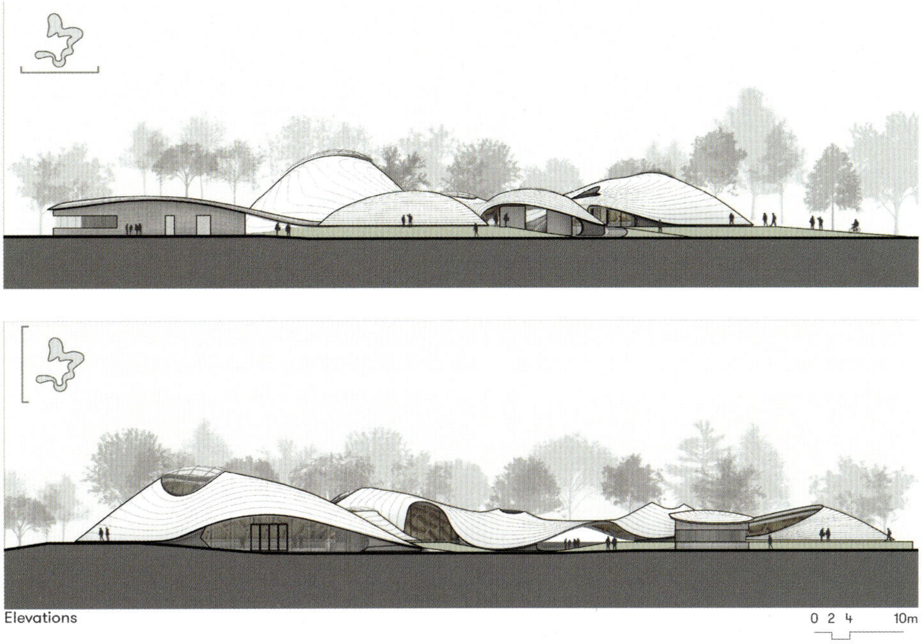

Elevations

Sections

Project behind the trees

Bridge of Nine Terraces

Perspective view of the project

Architect firm: Scenic Architecture Office
Principal architect: Zhu Xiaofeng
Design team: Zhou Yan (project architect), Li Qitong (project manager)
Location: Jiangsu Province, China
Completion date: 2022
Photography: Liang Shan

Located at the northern face of Xian Mountain, the Horticultural Expo Village is set in the northern part of the 11th Horticultural Expo Park in Nanjing, Jiangsu Province, China. A courtyard hotel has been constructed in the Expo Village—operated by VOCO—together with a farmland pavilion and a covered pedestrian bridge. Crossing Qixiang River from the north to the south, the Bridge of Nine Terraces provides a walking pathway into the Expo Village, with the mountains behind unfolding into view as visitors cross the bridge.

The design concept was driven mainly by two aspects. First, the space under the bridge needed to satisfy the height clearance for boats passing through. Considering the height difference between the revetment and the water level, the bridge needed to be raised in the middle. Second, as an important node, the bridge was imagined not only as a convenient access, but also as a place for visitors to gather, rest, and socialize. To fulfill these two conditions, the 8-meter-wide bridge deck has been divided into nine 4-by-8-meter platforms—like nine connected pavilions that gradually rise and fall. The most appropriate structural system to accommodate the concept was a big structural arch that suspends nine platforms. The folded plate, as a roof structure, achieves a large span, and also relates back to the spatial scale and form of the traditional dwellings in Jiangnan Region. Four steel trusses have been arranged and connected along the double gable roof to form a folded plate arch, which directs the vertical load of the suspended platforms to the two ends of the arch structure that extends a span of 37.8 meters.

Connected by ramps and steps along a central passage, the nine suspended platforms are light and permeable, accommodating seats for resting and counters or stands for selling wares. The terraces, with a height difference of only 300 millimeters between each other, are hung by 50-millimeter-diameter rods from the bottom of the folded plate truss arch to the overlapped part of the terraces. The overlapping enhances the stability of the terraces and enables each of them to have six hanging points with an interval of 4 meters. The terraces thus present a very thin structural thickness of 190 millimeters, and the distance between the bridge deck and the water surface is minimized. Bamboo curtains are hung between the rods to create a series of continuously staggered and vaguely partitioned spaces on the bridge like nine permeable cabins. The "slowness" nature of the bridge is thus interpreted and amplified.

The gravity and lateral thrust of the suspended terraces are finally passed on to the foundation on the revetment through two U-shaped concrete bridgeheads. The bridgeheads made of shear walls on both sides are simple and solid; the double gable roof extends to cover the shear walls, turning the bridgeheads into two semi-outdoor cabins, presenting an implied welcome of returning home.

Sitting on the bridge, one experiences the effect of wooden eaves that shade against the sunshine, bamboo curtains that filter light, and the scenery of the mountains and fields on either side extending into the distance along the river. By combining form-type and technology, the design bestows the bridge with a sense of homecoming, rest, and sightseeing, symbolically experienced through the "half houses" at the bridgeheads and through taking a leisurely walk down the suspended terraces.

Aerial view from the east

View from the riverbank

Plan

Terraces and activities

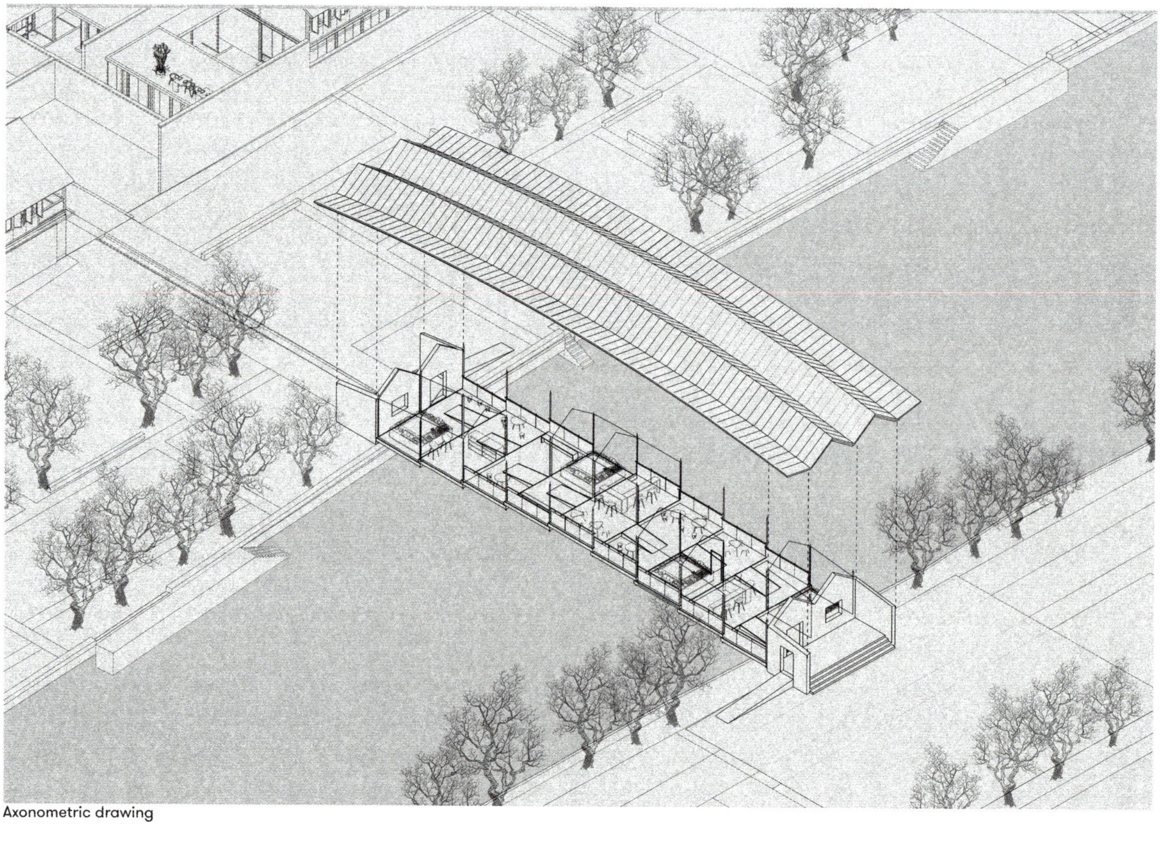
Axonometric drawing

View on the bridge

The bamboo curtains

Hole in bridge head

Vaguely partitioned spaces on the bridge

View on the bridge

1. 0.8-mm-thick titanium-zinc T50 vertical seaming plate
   6mm ventilation and noise reduction screen
   1.2-mm-thick self-adhesive waterproof membrane
   1.0-mm-thick galvanized leveling steel plate
   0.6-mm-thick galvanized profiled steel sheet
   Rectangular tube keel 80 mm × 80 mm × 3 mm
2. CLT spruce high-grade solid wood board
3. White stainless-steel metal mesh
4. White sling, anti-rust
5. Decorative bamboo curtain
6. Φ 8 mm black titanium 316 stainless-steel rod
7. 30 mm × 125 mm bamboo floor with a gap of 4mm
   Steel structure bridge deck with white fluorocarbon coating

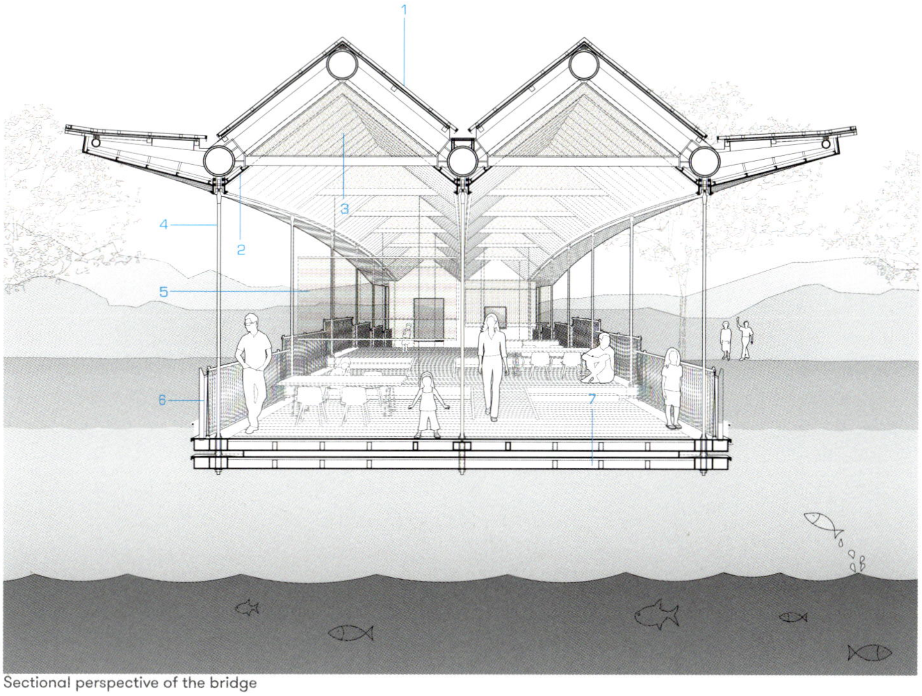

Sectional perspective of the bridge

Bridge head

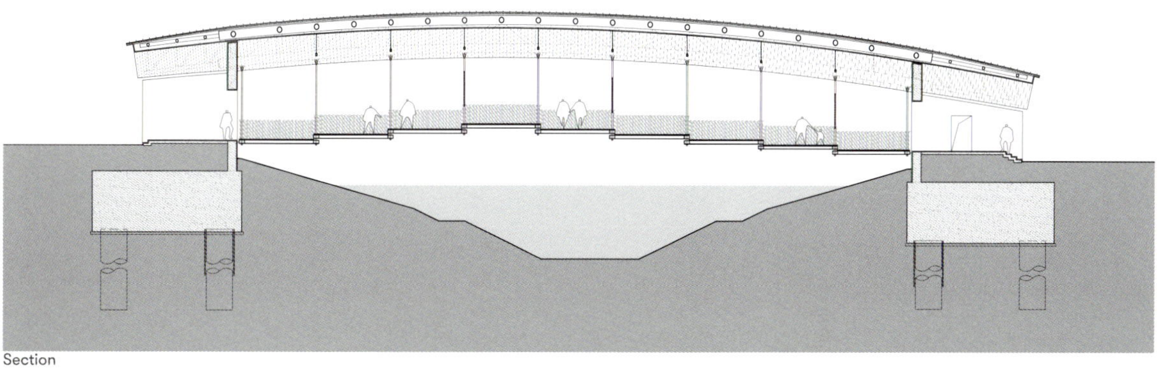
Section

Growing Up

North elevation

Architect firm: New Office Works
Principal architect: Paul Tse and Evelyn Ting
Design team: Paul Tse, Evelyn Ting, Julian Wong
Structural consultant: (Competition stage 2) Burohappold Engineering / Victoria Janssens, Christoph Tritschler
Roof cladding consultant: (Competition stage 2) Front Inc. / Evan Levelle
Structural consultant: (Technical design) Simon Pickard
Location: Hong Kong, China
Area: 240 square meters
Completion date: February 2019
Photography: Xu Liang Leon, Kris Provoost

Growing Up is a timber pavilion located along the West Kowloon Cultural District waterfront. It was the winner of the inaugural Hong Kong Young Architects & Designers Competition in 2017, selected out of 320 submissions by an expert panel of local and international jurors. Built as a temporary pavilion and opened for public enjoyment since 2019, it has become a recognisable venue for picnics and informal events with sweeping views of Victoria Harbour.

Just like how growing trees require good soil, growing culture requires a strong foundation of the city's collective memories. Growing Up captures everyday elements fundamental to Hong Kong, embedding and cultivating them within the fabric of a soon-to-be major arts and cultural center. A large, sloped roof is supported by a series of timber columns that, like the seedlings in the adjacent nursery park, grow from an intimate human scale to the harbour scale. A stepped landscape below, reminiscent of the city's hilly topography, provides both seating and stage for different activities.

"The design process was really an exercise in close observation of things around us, and (on) how to lend significance to various elements that comprise the city—steps, walkways, the way different roofs shed rainwater, (and) palm trees)," said Ms Evelyn Ting, Co-founder of New Office Works.

Despite its simple volume, each angle of the pavilion reveals a different sense of porosity, materiality, and scale. The north and south elevations are characterized by transparency, the surrounding trees a seamless backdrop between the pavilion's slender columns. However, as one moves around and the columns overlap in perspective, the pavilion edge becomes more solid and frames the waterfront view. The pavilion appears the most dense from the east, the structure of the steps forming an intricate screen to accentuate the transition from park to waterfront. In contrast, an open gathering space and distinct profile emerges from the harbor.

East elevation from nursery park

Aerial view of curved acrylic roof cladding

West elevation

South elevation

Pavilion interior

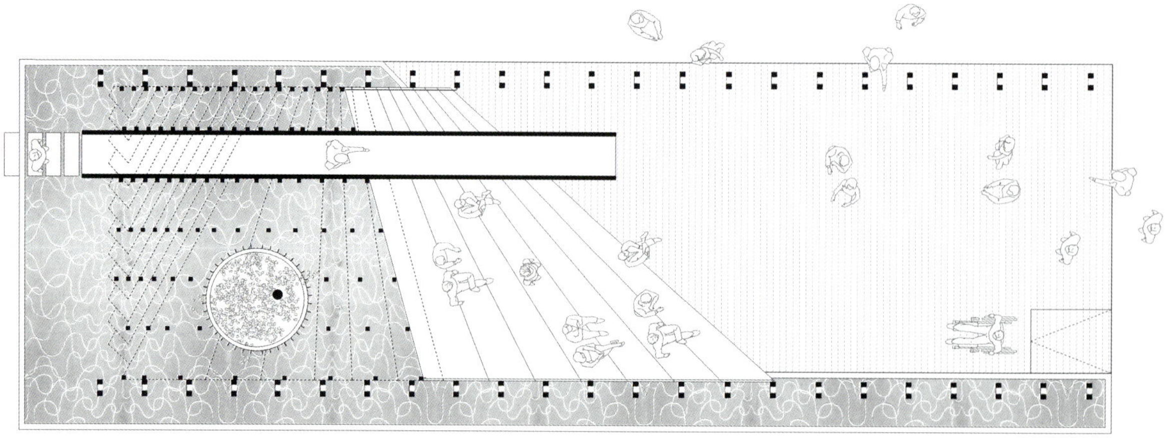

Floor plan

Entrance tunnel

East elevation with sunset view

Section

Hong Kong Palace Museum

Hong Kong Palace Museum

Architect firm: Rocco Design Architects Associates Ltd
Principal architect: Rocco Yim
Design team: Rocco Yim, C. M. Chan, Freddie Hai, Hoi-Wai Sze, Ryan Leong, William Lee, Kwong-Kiu Wong, Qingyue Li, Doris Yue, Samuel Wong, Bong Yeung, Thomas Cheng, Elaine Tsui, Felix Chow, Pak-Chuen Chan, Victor Chu
Location: Hong Kong, China
Area: 17,223 square meters
Completion date: September 2021
Photography: Rocco Design, Edmon Leong, Thomas Cheng Xiao, Hong Kong Palace Museum, Freeman Lau

Hong Kong Palace Museum is a flagship project of the West Kowloon Cultural District (WKCD) development. As a new center for Chinese art and antiquities in Hong Kong, the building will be home to more than 800 objects from the Beijing Palace Museum in the Forbidden City, including 160 Class A artefacts considered national treasures. The building is conceived as a civic hub and a new landmark for Hong Kong, as well as a platform to connect new generations with China's cultural history. It also hosts interactive and experiential exhibitions, casting a new light on antiquities.

The 30,000-square-meter building sits at the western tip of WKCD, adjacent to the Art Park, where it commands sweeping views over Victoria Harbor. The design embraces the spirit of bringing Chinese heritage to modern audiences, reinterpreting ancient Chinese spatial concepts in a contemporary architectural language. Based on the notion of spatial exploration through sequential courtyards in the Beijing Palace itself, Hong Kong Palace Museum stacks three atria that draw visitors up through the building. The vertical stacking references Hong Kong's dense and compact urban fabric, and also preserves as much open space and landscaped areas on the ground level as possible.

The three atriums offer panoramic vistas of the city and the surroundings in different directions. The entrance atrium is orientated toward the east, with a vista toward the Xiqu Center at the eastern end of the West Kowloon Cultural District. The South Atrium and outdoor viewing deck are rotated toward the south, offering visitors commanding views of Hong Kong's iconic skyline, and has become one of the museum's most Instagrammable spots. The uppermost Western Atrium is rotated toward the west, with views of Lantau Island and the South China Sea in the distance. The atria make the social heart of the museum, and guests can gather here to discuss the art on display, enjoy views that graze far across the surroundings, or simply sit in quietude to contemplate the art they have seen. They can experience the city in an unparalleled way.

Approaching the building, visitors pass through a grand elevated plaza that can host installations and stage performances of traditional ceremonies and dance. The museum's entrance pavilion frames the plaza, recalling the gates of the Forbidden City. Beyond, guests enter a vast lobby where they can relax, chat, and learn about the exhibitions on display.

An undulating bronze ceiling articulates the space, referencing the gold Beijing Palace roofs. It unfolds to accompany a circulation spine that extends the full height of the building, in turn enhancing vertical connectivity and bringing natural light streaming down from above. This ceiling acts as an orientating and sculptural element, adding accent to the space's refined palette of stone and polished concrete walls and floors.

The spine winds through five levels of galleries that offer 7,800 square meters of total exhibition space. The galleries display a collection of objects from as early as the Jin dynasty (AD 226–420), as well as painting, calligraphy, rare books, and decorative art like gold, bronze, and jade items.

While most of the galleries house long-term displays, a double-height thematic gallery on the fourth floor houses exhibits that are rotated frequently, and promotes innovative curatorial experiences, including participatory and technologically enhanced exhibitions. This is also a venue where treasures from different countries—including exhibits from the Louvre in the opening exhibition—can be displayed in dialog with the treasures of Beijing.

The museum also includes a 400-seat auditorium that hosts public programs and film screenings, activity rooms, and a ground-floor restaurant and shop that create an active edge on the Art Park and harborfront walkways.

Hong Kong Palace Museum

Main entrance lobby

Second-floor atrium

Hong Kong Palace Museum

Second-floor atrium

Fourth-floor West Atrium

Fourth-floor West Atrium

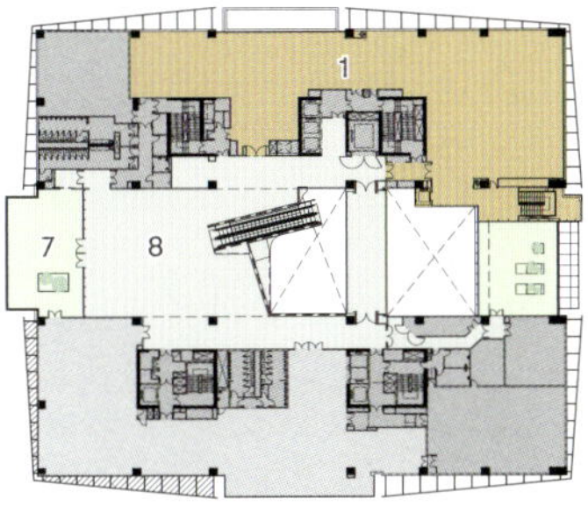

Fourth-floor plan

Second-floor plan

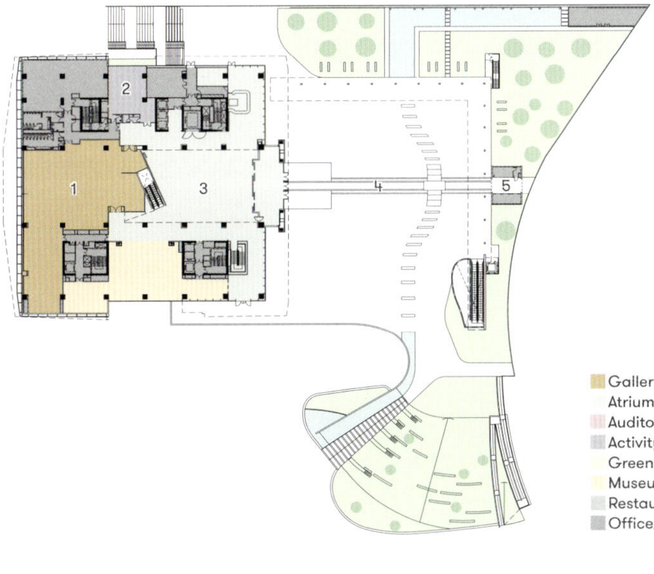

Ground-floor plan

- Gallery
- Atrium
- Auditorium
- Activity Room
- Greenery Deck
- Museum Shop
- Restaurant
- Office/Back of house

1. Gallery
2. Scholar's Commons
3. GF Lobby
4. Museum Plaza
5. Tickets
6. South Atrium
7. Viewing Deck
8. West Atrium

Fourth-floor Atrium

Skylight and Featured Bronze Ceiling above the atria

Gallery 9

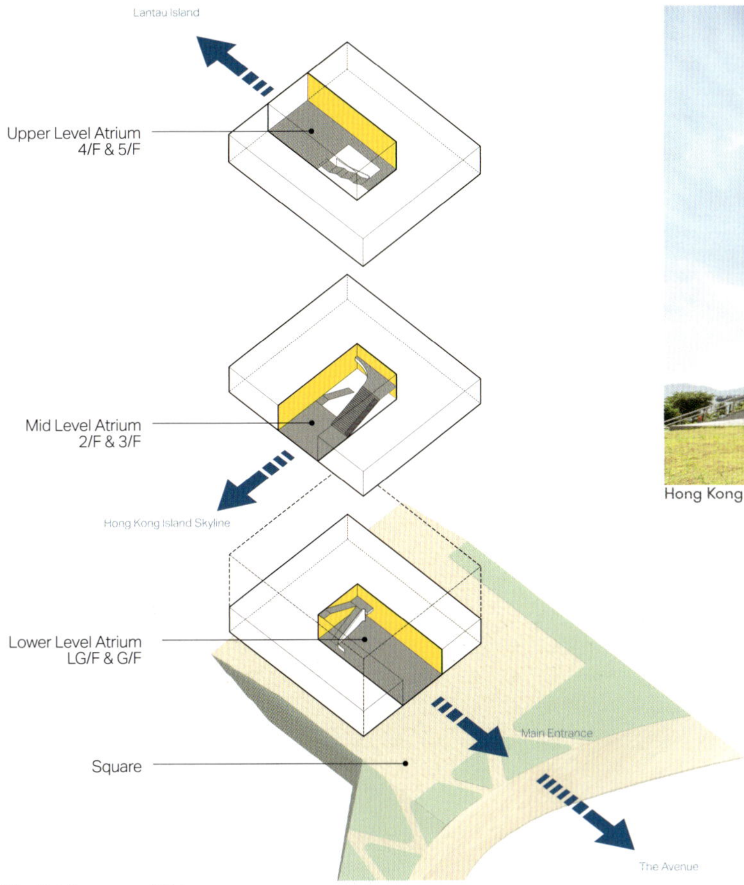

Vertical Spatial Sequence of Atria

Hong Kong Palace Museum

1. Museum Restaurant
2. Learning Resource Center
3. The Hong Kong Jockey Club Auditorium
4. Gallery 1
5. GF Lobby
6. South Atrium
7. Viewing Deck
8. West Atrium

- Gallery
- Atrium
- Auditorium
- Activity Room
- Greenery Deck
- Museum Shop
- Restaurant
- Office/Back of house

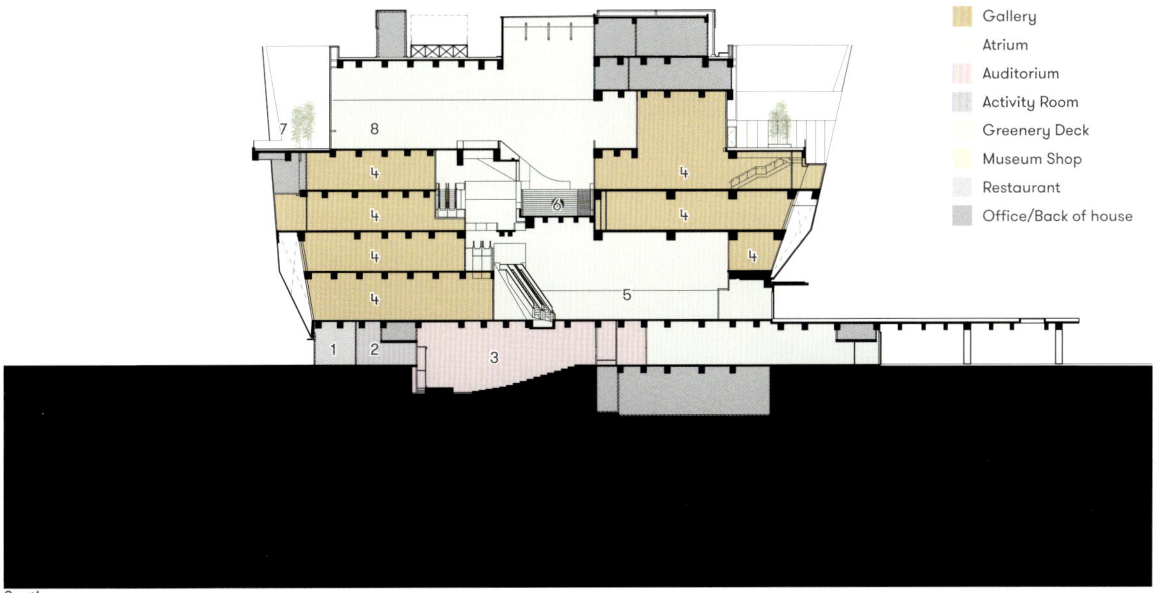

Section

M+ Museum of Visual Culture, an Iconic Cultural Destination for Asia and Beyond

Façade facing the Victoria Harbour © Virgile Simon Bertrand

Architect firm: Herzog & de Meuron in partnership with TFP Farrells and Arup
Principal architect: Herzog & de Meuron
Design team:
Herzog & de Meuron, TFP Farrells, Arup
Location: Hong Kong, China
Area: Approx 87,400 square meters
Completion date: February 2021
Photography: Kevin Mak, Kris Provoost, Virgile Simon Bertrand

M+ Museum of Visual Culture, Asia's first global museum of contemporary visual culture in Hong Kong, opened to the public in November 2021. A cultural center for twentieth- and twenty-first-century art, design, architecture, and moving image, the 65,000-square-meter building houses 17,000 square meters of exhibition space across thirty-three typologically varying galleries. It also includes three cinemas, the Mediatheque, Learning Hub, Research Center, museum shops, restaurants, a tea and coffee bar, a members lounge, and office spaces, with a roof garden that commands spectacular views of Victoria Harbour.

Rooted in the ground of the reclaimed land, the building rises up to the sky with its face toward the city. Along with the Conservation and Storage Facility (CSF) and WKCDA Tower, M+ Museum of Visual Culture is one of Hong Kong's latest landmarks shaping the emerging West Kowloon Cultural District, expressing a vision for a new institution of visual culture for Hong Kong and the world.

The building is composed of a slender tower raised atop a square podium. Seen from the outside, the monolithic form and austere elegance of the building allow it to both define a unique presence on Victoria Harbour and remain in dialogue with the surrounding cityscape. The podium and tower are united as concrete structures clad in ceramic tiles that reflect the changing conditions of light and weather, while standing out from nearby glass and steel skyscrapers. The tower façade also features an LED system for the display of artwork, which are mostly specially commissioned and relate to the museum exhibitions, making a distinctive contribution to the city's vibrant nighttime environment. This presents a large welcoming image across the harbour.

On entering the museum, visitors experience the bright, open qualities of the interior, which include a central lightwell and an excavated exhibition space named Found Space, which follows the contours of the underground Airport Express railway tunnel. Initially a challenge to the construction works, it inspired the design of the building and became a large found space anchoring the museum in the ground.

The expansive podium, which houses a public roof garden and a sequence of display spaces, cantilevers above the ground floor to provide generous shelter and shade along the building perimeter throughout the year. The multiple entrances to the building allow for a porous system of spaces and encourage a sense of openness to the surrounding environment. Thus, the building has a very low threshold—it's a public space both inside and out and a social space for people. This makes the encounter with art easier, and ultimately more democratic. Details such as the façade's custom-designed cladding, inspired by traditional Chinese roofs, and the differently textured wood and concrete used across the museum's interiors reveal the architects' innovative adoption of vernacular design elements and the use of durable materials.

The M+ Museum of Visual Culture incorporates the latest proven technologies and has adopted sustainability as a core principle in its development, with the goal of becoming a "low carbon and low energy" landmark venue in the district. With a unified vision to achieve carbon neutrality in the long term, Integrated Sustainable Building Design (ISBD) was applied across all areas and disciplines of building design. The building provides a high-quality environment whilst significantly reducing energy and potable water consumption. The roof garden provides a publicly accessible, landscaped garden that capitalizes on the local microclimate that is refreshed by the harbour breeze. Internally, skylights allow daylight to filter through and animate selected gallery spaces, reducing the need for artificial lighting. Architectural shading on the façade minimizes heat gain and energy needed for cooling. The remaining building loads are served by district cooling and supplemented by solar hot water panels to reduce energy consumption. The completed M+ building and WKCDA Tower have both achieved the "Gold" rating under BEAM Plus Assessment.

The M+ building, viewed from the Victoria Harbour © Kevin Mak

Entrance © Kevin Mak

Stairs © Kris Provoost

Main hall © Kevin Mak

Main hall © Kevin Mak

Found space © Iwan Baan

Atrium on the second floor © Kris Provoost

Gallery space © Iwan Baan

Gallery space © Iwan Baan

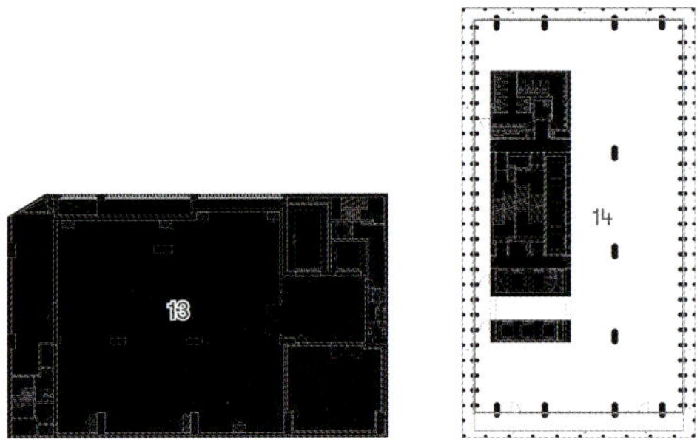

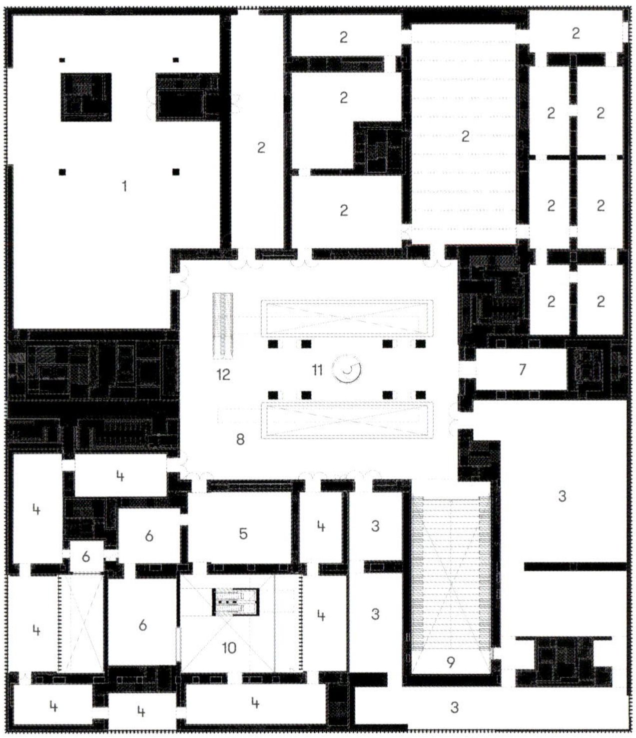

1. West Gallery
2. Sigg Galleries
3. East Galleries
4. South Galleries
5. The Cabinet
6. Courtyard Galleries
7. Focus Gallery
8. Atrium
9. Grand Stair
10. Courtyard
11. Spiral Staircase to Terrace Restaurant
12. Escalator from G/F Main Hall
13. M+ Ancillary Building (CSF Building)
14. WKCDA Tower

Second-floor plan © Herzog & de Meuron

Landscape podium © Kevin Mak

Horizon Terrace © Kris Provoost

1. Found Space
2. The Studio
3. Main Hall
4. Atrium
5. Galleries
6. Terrace Restaurant
7. Research Center
8. Office
9. M+ Members Lounge
10. Art-related OACF
11. RDE (F&B)
12. Roof Garden
13. CSF Building Art Storage
14. CSF Building Conservation Labs
15. Avenue
16. Carriageway
17. Parking
18. Waterfront Promenade
19. Victoria Harbour
20. Airport Express Line Tunnel
21. MTR/Elements Cooling Main

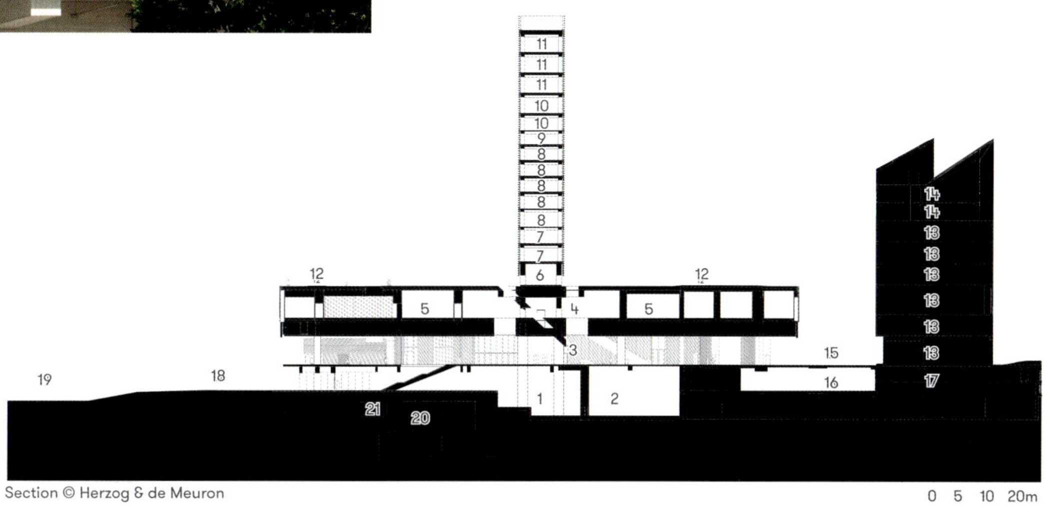

Section © Herzog & de Meuron

Xiqu Center

The stunning Xiqu Centre celebrates Chinese Opera through its dynamic, glowing façade and striking moon gate, reminiscent of a lantern shimmering behind a beaded stage curtain
© Ema Peter

Architect firm: Revery Architecture Inc. in joint venture with Ronald Lu & Partners Ltd.
Principal architect: Revery Architecture — Bing THOM (deceased 2016), Venelin KOKALOV, Earle BRIGGS, Francis YAN (deceased 2018); Ronald Lu & Partners — Dr. Ronald LU, Bryant LU, Andy LEUNG, Peter YAM
Location: West Kowloon Cultural District, Hong Kong, China
Area: 28,162 square meters
Completion date: November 2018
Photography: Ronald Lu & Partners

Xiqu Center is the first landmark performance venue for the West Kowloon Cultural District. The stunning, award-winning center was created to celebrate the ancient art of traditional Chinese Opera and has become a new landmark for Hong Kong's built environment. At first sight, the building immediately conveys the beauty of Chinese Opera culture through its dynamic, glowing façade and striking moon gate, reminiscent of a lantern shimmering behind a beaded stage curtain.

Epitomizing culture, sustainability, accessibility, and human centricity, the design of Xiqu Center was a joint venture by Revery Architecture and Ronald Lu & Partners (RLP Asia). The seven-story building houses a 1,075-seat Grand Theater, a Tea House Theater, with around 200 seats, eight professional studios, a seminar hall, and two floors of retail and dining space that have balconies overlooking a central inner courtyard.

The façade's intricate woven metal panels are gently pulled back like curtains at all four corners of the building, radiating light out to the exterior to welcome visitors into the interior plaza. The concept of *qi* or flow, is expressed throughout, through curvilinear paths and forms and arched entrances designed around the multilevel circular atrium. The moon gate is comprised of a modular system of scaled fins made from untreated marine-grade aluminum piping that is arranged in alternating patterns along the front of the building.

Inside, the remarkable Grand Theater is suspended aboveground, elevated by 27 meters to create ample space beneath for the enormous atrium. It also isolates the theater from the noise and vibrations of the surrounding city.

Large openings in the façade and a passive ventilation chimney produce a natural stack effect. Aided by prevailing winds and augmented by trees and diffused natural light, the ambient temperature in the plaza is significantly lower than that of the surrounding urban area, providing heat relief to patrons and visitors passing through. The atrium also serves as a public plaza for exhibitions, stalls, and Chinese Opera demonstrations and workshops. This open yet covered exterior space is not air-conditioned—which is a unique characteristic for a public space in Hong Kong's humid, subtropical climate. The area is a passively cooled, comfortable, and inclusive "urban living room" for the community that is always accessible.

Sustainability considerations were incorporated throughout the center's design and construction. A comprehensive construction waste management scheme reduced waste by 60 per cent, and modular components were used wherever possible: the ceiling and cladding in the public areas are all modular, and the façade is made of interchangeable fins and unitised modules, all of which produced near-zero waste during installation. Regionally and sustainably sourced wood-based materials and recycled timber products were also used, further reducing waste and lowering the project's overall carbon footprint.

Prioritizing accessibility, Xiqu Center has also been designed to welcome people at all times of the day and in all weather conditions. It is connected to two mass transit stations and is easily accessed by public transport from all parts of Hong Kong. With its strategic location next to the Express Rail Terminus, it is an arts hub serving more than the Hong Kong community to also include patrons from the whole Greater Bay Area.

This new icon for Hong Kong's glittering West Kowloon Cultural District keeps the art of Cantonese Opera alive and thriving for the enjoyment and appreciation of many generations of people today, tomorrow, and long into the future.

Located in the West Kowloon Cultural District, the Xiqu Centre has become a new Hong Kong landmark

The façade's woven metal panels are pulled back like curtains at the building's corners, radiating light into the exterior

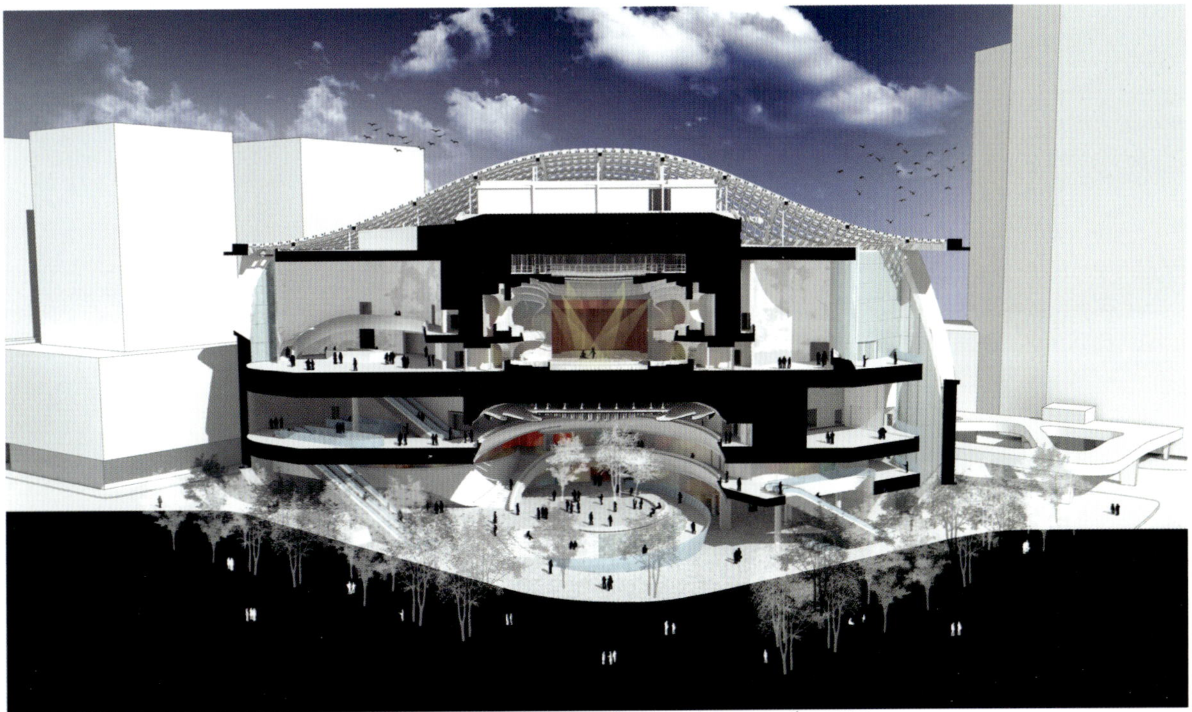

The seven-storey building houses a 1,075-seat Grand Theatre, a 200-seat Tea House Theatre and numerous other spaces

The plaza is a passively cooled, covered exterior space incorporating trees, natural ventilation, and diffused natural light

The Grand Theatre is elevated 27 meters above ground, creating a public atrium used for exhibitions, demonstrations, and workshops © West Kowloon Cultural District Authority

The concept of *qi* or "flow", is expressed throughout the building through curvilinear paths and forms © Kevin Mak

Strategic openings and portals take advantage of natural cooling from prevailing winds © Kevin Mak

The plaza creates a cool and comfortable "urban living room" for the community © Ema Peter

The Xiqu Centre conveys the beauty of Chinese Opera culture, epitomising culture, sustainability, accessibility, and human centricity

Regionally- and sustainably-sourced wood-based materials and recycled timber products are used throughout

The suspended Grand Theatre is isolated from the noise and vibrations of the surrounding city © Ema Peter

The West Kowloon Cultural District: An Ambitious Vision Taking Shape

West Kowloon Cultural District. Courtesy of West Kowloon Cultural District Authority

Thomas Chung, HKIA, RIBA
Guest Editor
Associate Professor, The Chinese University of Hong Kong
Photography: WKCD Authority, Han Man

Hong Kong's West Kowloon Cultural District (WKCD) represents an exciting and ambitious vision to transform 40 hectares of reclaimed land into a world-class arts and entertainment district. After over two decades of planning and development, this HK$29 billion project is finally starting to take shape, with the recent openings of long-awaited landmark venues like the M+ Museum of Visual Culture, the Xiqu Center and the Hong Kong Palace Museum showcasing the city's design prowess on an international stage.

The WKCD's scale and scope are undeniably impressive. By bringing together an array of cultural facilities - from performing arts theaters to museums housing expansive collections - the district aims to cement Hong Kong's status as a global hub for the arts. Its recent architecture is characterized by a blend of variegated contemporaneity, cultural relevance, and welcoming publicness. The Hong Kong Palace Museum elegantly reimagines Chinese spatial traditions in a modern language, while the M+, Museum of Visual Culture, offers a striking juxtaposition of a monolithic form with a vibrant LED façade. The lantern-inspired Xiqu Center, with its intricate woven metal panels and moon gate, celebrates the beauty of traditional Chinese opera. As a counterpoint to these monumental venues, the Growing Up pavilion, whose simple yet impactful design captures elements of Hong Kong's urban fabric, is an inviting open structure made almost entirely in timber.

The WKCD's drawn-out trajectory has not been without its challenges. Early design proposals were scrapped after intense public scrutiny, while ballooning budgets raised concerns about governance and oversight. Nevertheless, the WKCD Authority has certainly demonstrated resilience, and has been adjusting plans to better reflect local needs and priorities. Now, as the mega arts hub's architectural icons and well-designed public landscapes are opened, the true test lies ahead. Besides offering fantastic harbourfront views and ample public parkspace, can the WKCD's programming and curation captivate both Hong Kongers and international visitors? Will it strike the right balance between celebrating local artistic voices and attracting global talent?

With its world-class architecture and state-of-the-art facilities, the WKCD holds immense potential to enrich Hong Kong's cultural landscape. If successfully cultivated as a vibrant precinct with boundary-pushing arts incubators, it could consolidate the city's reputation as an international cultural destination for Asia and beyond. With the Hong Kong International Cultural Summit staged in March 2024 as a first attempt to foster long-term exchanges and partnerships between the local and global arts community, it is hoped that the genuine commitment to serving the city's cultural aspirations perseveres as the district seeks to fulfill its grand vision.

M+ view of public space

M+ overview (Courtesy of West Kowloon Cultural District Authority)

Art Park, looking south towards Hong Kong island. Courtesy of West Kowloon Cultural District Authority

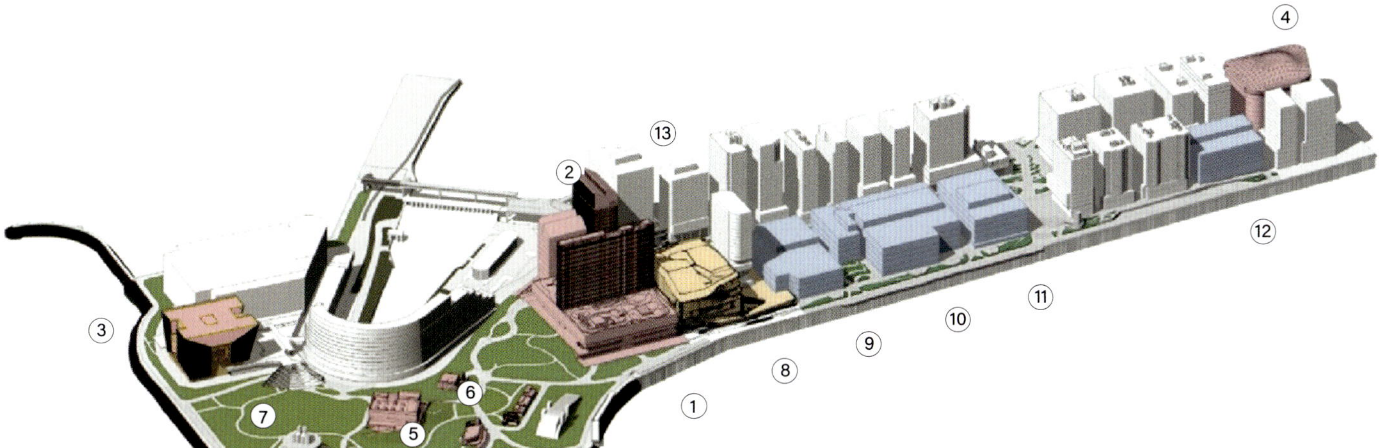

Completed Arts and Cultural Facilities (ACF)
ACF under construction
Batch 3 ACF (subject to funding availability and review)
Commercial Development / ACF

1. M+
2. WKCDA Tower & Conservation and Storage Facility
3. Hong Kong Palace Museum
4. Xiqu Center
5. Freespace
6. Arts Pavilion
7. Art Park
8. Lyric Theater Complex
(including Lyric Theater, Medium Theater & Studio Theater)
9. Music Center
10. Great Theater
11. Musical Theater
12. Medium Theater
13. Three Artist Square Towers

WestK Design Concept and Development Plan from Foster + Partners: City Park: Green; Free; Liveable; Walkable; Sustainable. Courtesy of West Kowloon Cultural District Authority

Hong Kong Palace Museum. Courtesy of West Kowloon Cultural District Authority

Hong Kong Palace Museum

Tai Kwun—Central Police Station Revitalization Project

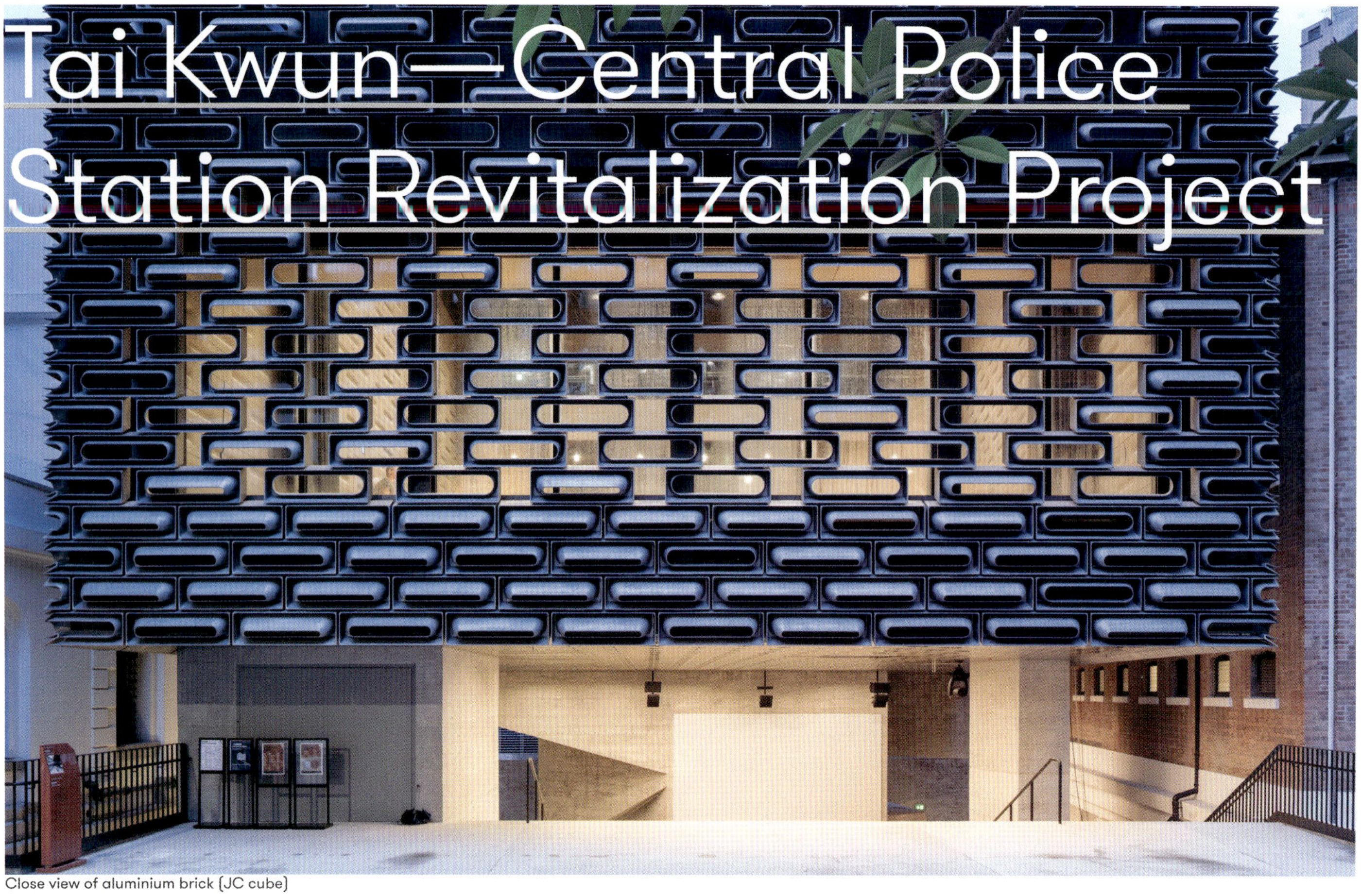

Close view of aluminium brick (JC cube)

Architect firm: Rocco Design Architects Limited (in association with Herzog & de Meuron and Purcell)
Principal architect: Rocco Yim
Design team: Rocco Yim, Bernard Hui, CM Chan, Charles Kung, David Chan, Cecilia Tam, Angela Fong, Tong Hui Ching, Becky Luk, Winnie Man, Denis Tsang, Sandra Leung
Location: Hong Kong, China
Area: 14,500 square meters
Completion date: 2018
Photography: Tai Kwun, Iwan Baan, Rocco Design

Tai Kwun—The Central Police Station (CPS) Revitalization Project consists of three "Declared Monuments"—the former Central Police Station, the Central Magistracy, and Victoria Prison, sixteen historical buildings, and two new buildings. The synergy of the new and heritage buildings, together with publicly accessible outdoor spaces, offer broad civic appeal and provide intimate, multipurpose venues for visual and performing arts activities. It has become a key gathering place in Central where a diverse community can partake in and enjoy leisure and cultural elements.

The revitalization project was led by The Hong Kong Jockey Club, in partnership with the Government of the Hong Kong SAR. The highest standards of heritage conservation have been applied at Tai Kwun, with unfailing attention to authenticity. In contrast to the heritage buildings' respective original functions as a police station, court room, and prison, they are instead now on full display, giving the public the chance to appreciate up-close their contrasting architectural features and fine design details.

Once a highly secured compound surrounded by high granite walls, the revitalization of Central Police Station embeds the site back into the city, including Lan Kwai Fong, Soho and other precincts, while retaining the historic walls with strategic new entrances. The Central-Mid-level escalators connect with the Parade Ground and three platforms at different levels within site are connected via a newly formed Tai Kwun Lane that penetrates the site in the north-south direction, with new link bridges and lifts, allowing barrier free access.

Having gone through the necessary statutory approvals, Tai Kwun has established an exemplar for the adaptive reuse of heritage buildings, with innovative responses in various design aspects to minimize the visual and physical impact on historic fabrics while maintaining current city code requirements.

The new buildings are presented in a contemporary style, with a façade treatment that echoes the patterns of existing stone walls, providing a distinctive architectural feature as a contrast to the existing heritage fabric.

Parade Ground

Prism yard (west)

Aerial view of Tai Kwun

Connecting bridge, Tai Kwun Lane

Entrance of JC Contemporary

Prism yard (east)

Laundry steps (as outdoor theater)

Spiral stair (JC contemporary)

Stairwell, East Hall

Headquarter black

New footbridge connecting mid-level escalator

Arbuthnot road (east elevation)

Siu Hei Court Play Space

Siu Hei Court Play Space

Architect firm: One Bite Design Studio
Principal architect: One Bite Design Studio
Design team: Alan Cheung, Eleanor Fu, Sarah Mui, Melody Siu, Tony Zhang
Location: Siu Hei Court, Tuen Mun, Hong Kong, China
Area: 4,000 square meters
Completion date: 2020
Photography: Gaw Capital—People's Place and Tai Ngai Lung

In each placemaking project, One Bite Design Studio (onebie) takes a proactive approach to study each community's needs, identifying gaps where design interventions can foster positive community development through collaboration with clients.

Siu Hei Court Play Space, an intergenerational area with family-friendly recreational facilities, exemplifies this approach.

Located atop a multi-story carpark managed by Gaw Capital/People's Place (GC/PP), Siu Hei Court Play Space showcases a design that aims to strengthen community identity. It also rejuvenates the rooftop to become an attractive space for the residents of the surrounding public residences. Inspired by the homonym Siu Hei, signifying joy and laughter, the design concept embraces a theme of happiness that is rooted in the estate's history and local culture.

The result is a playful, multifunctional space which exudes vibrancy with bright colors, custom typography, and witty taglines that elicit smiles. Leveraging the potential of the rooftop as the "fifth façade," graphics have been designed on the ground to create visual interactions with residents living in the surrounding high-rise blocks. On one end are visible the letters "SH"—shorthand for Siu Hei—and on the other, the number "85"—the year Siu Hei Court was built. Hidden smiley faces on the play space also weave a vibe of positivity that draws both children and adults alike.

Taking advantage of the split-level roofscape, the lower level has been configured into a multifunctional play space, with court markings for basketball, badminton, and volleyball, a 150-meter-long running track, and a gridded playscape that encourages unstructured play for all ages.

The upper-level features basketball court markings arranged as one full-court and two half-courts, so basketball enthusiasts can hone their shooting skills and accuracy at various distances. A dual-direction spectator stand provides a shaded resting space that connects the two levels while offering a welcoming environment to gather at.

Aerial View of Siu Hei Court Play Space at Tuen Mun, Hong Kong

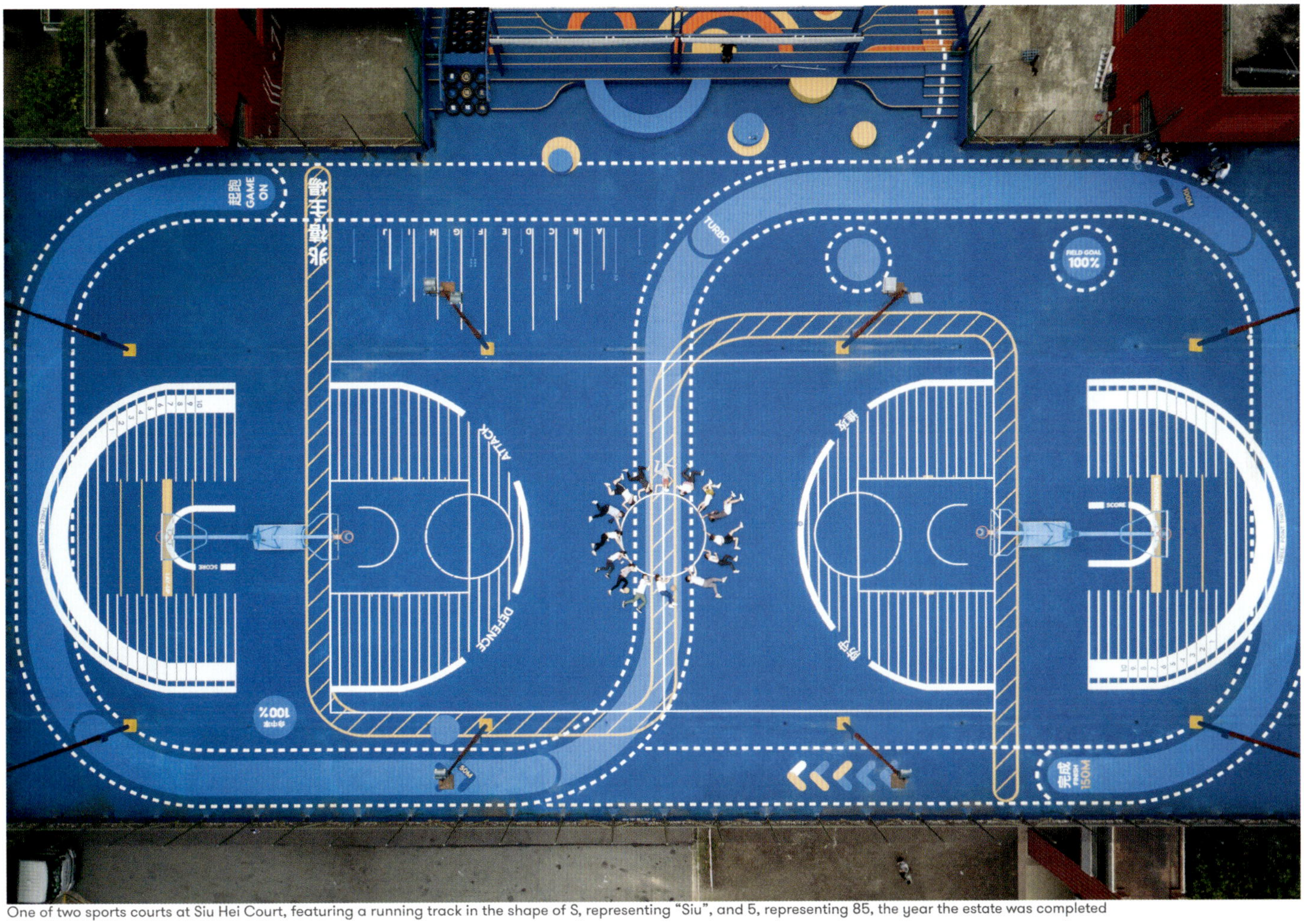

One of two sports courts at Siu Hei Court, featuring a running track in the shape of S, representing "Siu", and 5, representing 85, the year the estate was completed

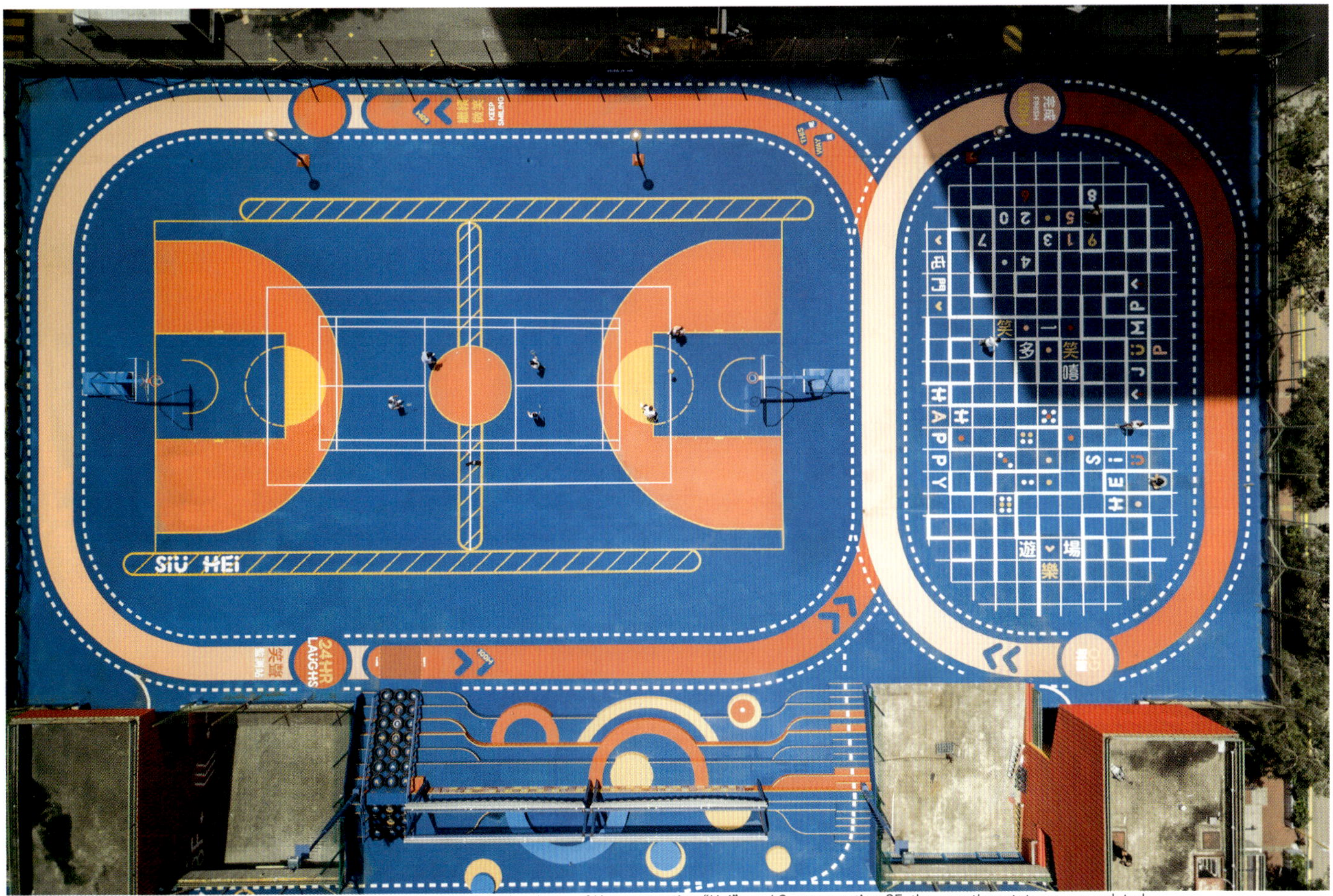

One of two playing courts at Siu Hei Court, featuring a running track in the shape of H, representing "Hei", and 8, representing 85, the year the estate was completed

Reminiscent of old playgrounds in Hong Kong, the car-tire installation at the spectator stand could be used as seats and as targets for shooting games; a rubberized EPDM platform provides additional grip for safety

Gridded playscape with witty colloquial slogans, which encourages unstructured play and leisure activities for all ages

Art by nearby kindergarten and primary school children is featured on the walls of the spectator stand

Ming Tak Sports Court

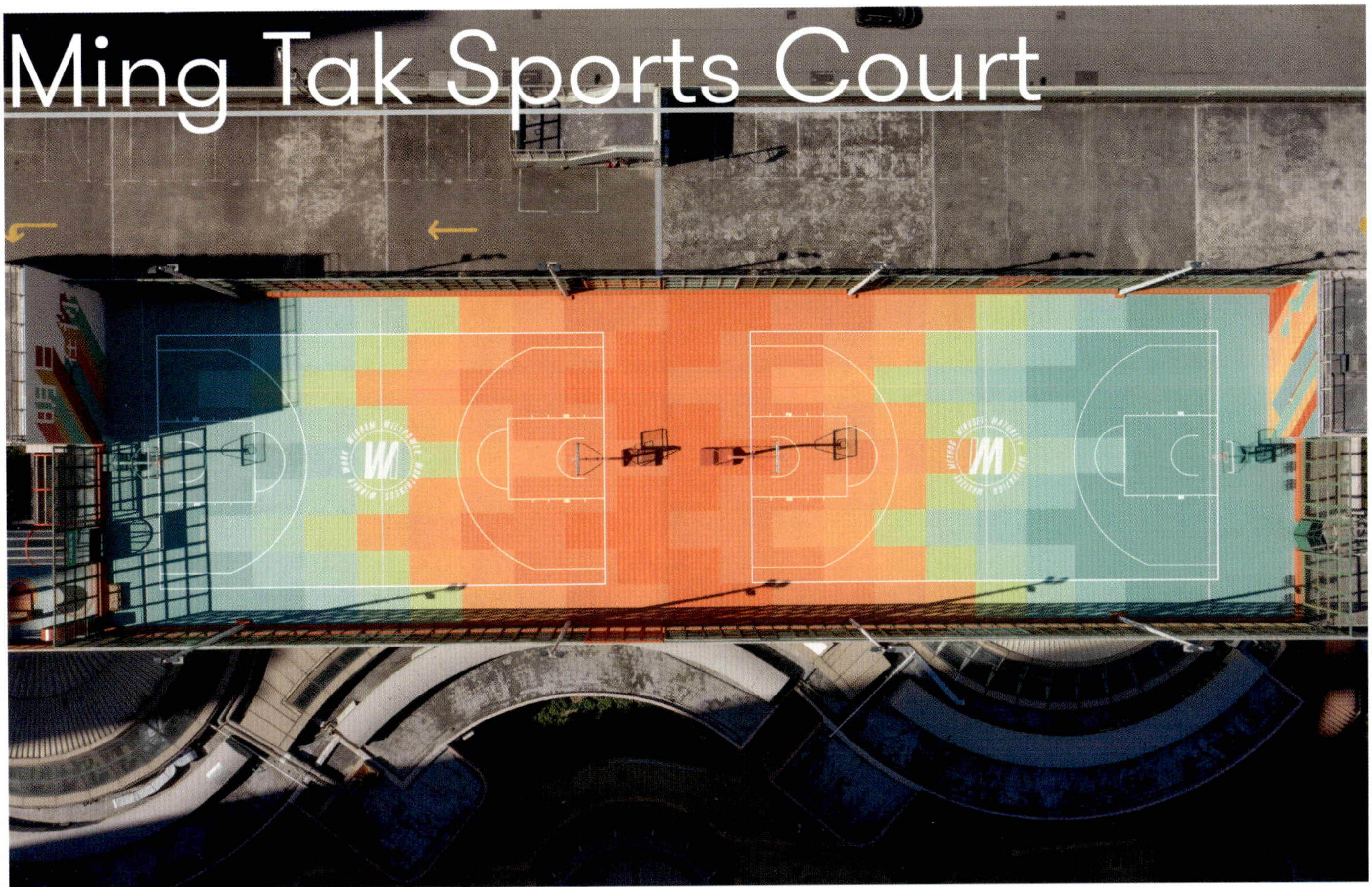

Aerial View of Ming Tak Sports Court at Tseung Kwan O, Hong Kong

Architect firm: One Bite Design Studio
Principal architect: One Bite Design Studio
Design team: Alan Cheung, Kary Chan, Sarah Mui, Melody Siu, Ryan Tung
Location: Ming Tak Estate, Tseung Kwan O, Hong Kong, China
Area: 1,400 square meters
Completion date: 2021
Photography: Gaw Capital, People's Place & Tai Ngai Lung

Placemaking aids in creating suitable public spaces that will bring the community out to live, work, play, and learn in. Each placemaking endeavour at One Bite Design Studio is unique, drawing upon local characteristics that will resonate with the community.

For the revamp of Ming Tak Sports Court, the aim was to encourage women's participation in sports. The design team worked with Gaw Capital/People's Place to create a appositive social message anchored in a design that motivates and moves the community while creating a sense of belonging and ownership. A pixelated, gradient floor pattern forms the letter "W" on one end and the letter "M" on the other to bring out the importance of gender diversity in sports.

Auxiliary amenities were also added, like hooks on railings for hanging personal belonging. The rest zone was also refurbished with make-up mirrors in keeping with female-friendly fittings that will help to create a welcoming environment for women. Sit-up benches and stretch bars complete the zone and extend various exercise opportunities that women will enjoy and can participate in comfortably.

The public space design incorporated motivational taglines for women during the revamp of Ming Tak Sports Court

Pixelated gradient floor pattern

Drawing from the first character of the estate's Chinese name "Ming Tak", the feature tagline for the sports court translates to "You create your future"

Revitalization of Sun Tin Wai Commercial Center

Aerial View of Sun Tin Wai Commercial Center's open-air courtyard, Sha Tin, Hong Kong

Architect firm: One Bite Design Studio
Principal architect: One Bite Design Studio
Design team: Alan Cheung, Eva Cheung, Lung Mak, Melody Siu, Sarah Mui, Sherene Ng
Location: Sun Tin Wai Estate, Sha Tin, Hong Kong, China
Area: 15,000 square meters
Completion date: 2020
Photography: Tai Ngai Lung

Double ageing poses a significant urban challenge in Hong Kong, China. It entails social and structural problems brought on by an ageing baby-boomer population and the ageing building stock built to accommodate them in the decades following World War II. One Bite Design Studio believes placemaking is a solution to sustain the functionality of ageing public housing estates using human-centered design strategies to amplify local identity, empower community champions, and implement solutions to create beloved public spaces.

The revitalization of Sun Tin Wai Commercial Center marks the studio's first collaboration with Sunlink Holdings (H.K.) Limited (SHHK). The design team drew inspiration from the estate's Chinese name, "Wai," which reflects a historical era when villages used tall walls for protection and created internal courtyards for communal activities.

To evoke this atmosphere and promote intergenerational bonding, the podium courtyard was repurposed into different activity zones that can host activities suitable for the whole family, such as community planting and fitness workouts. The furniture at the center is composed mainly of outdoor furniture and made up of movable pieces as well as specifically designed pieces, such as curved seats that create circles, so as to encourage social interaction.

Placemaking intertwines architectural design and human-centered solutions. Through different placemaking projects, One Bite Design Studio explores how the synergy between design and community can transform underused spaces. Through this, communities are empowered to use public spaces sustainably and forge social connections. Such placemaking revamps also draw people toward patronising local shops and participating in activities organized by place managers like GC/PP and SHHK. This forms a virtuous placemaking cycle where the more place managers contribute to the community, the more users will reciprocate and sustain place vibrancy.

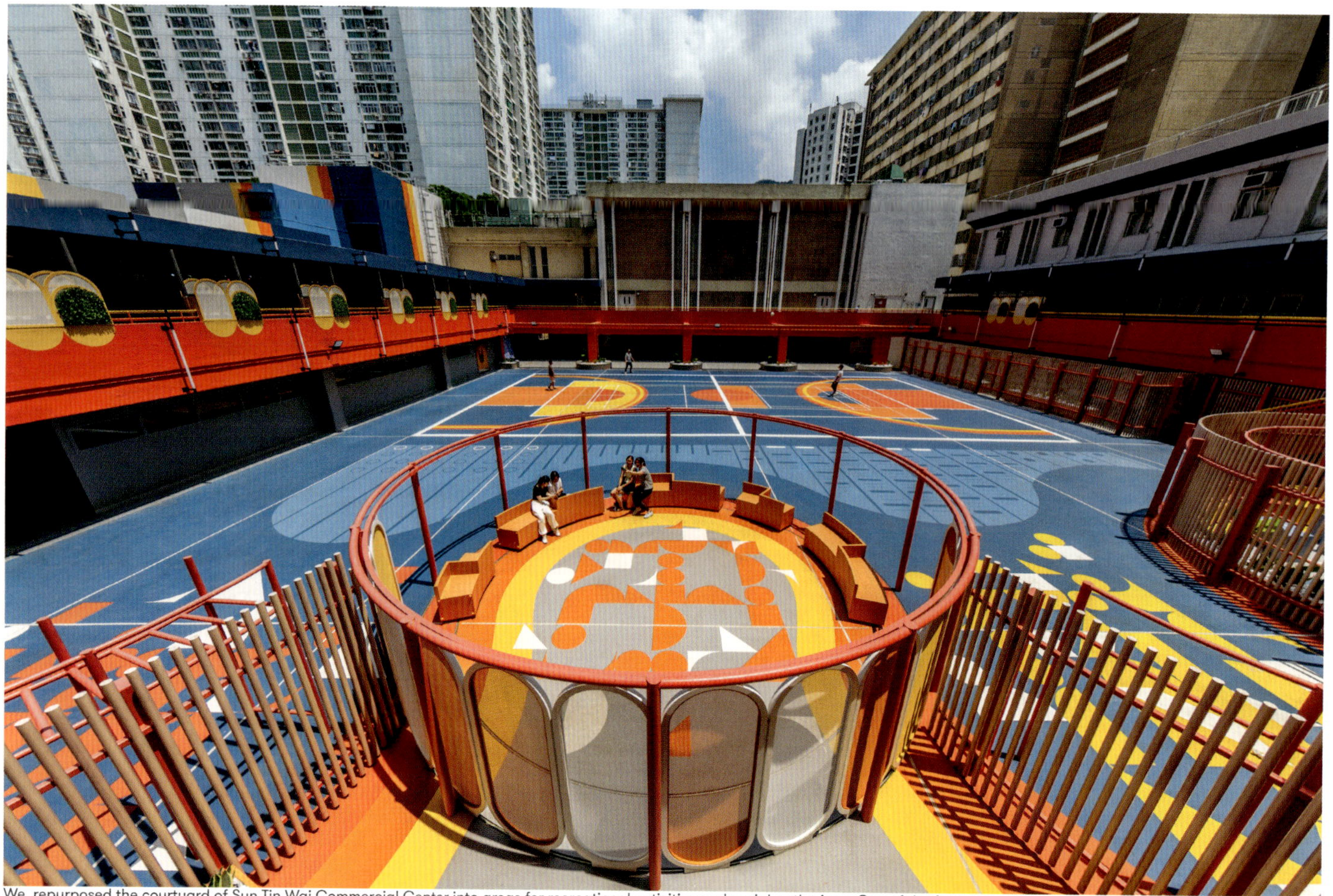

We repurposed the courtyard of Sun Tin Wai Commercial Center into areas for recreational activities and social gatherings. One of the four activity zones used galvanized mild steel (GMS) to create movable screens and fences which segmented the open-air area into smaller zones where groups of users could use the space to conduct multiple functions concurrently

GMS furniture in different shapes that users can move for flexible seating; they blend seamlessly with geometric motifs on the floor, creating a coherent visual identity for the courtyard space

TONGJI ARCHITECTURAL DESIGN (GROUP) CO., LTD.

Exterior of the TJAD office building

ABOUT TJAD

Tongji Architectural Design (Group) Co., Ltd. (TJAD), formerly known as the Architectural Design and Research Institute of Tongji University, was founded in 1958 and has now developed into a well-known large-scale design and consulting group.

Shanghai Museum East Hall

With almost seventy years of history behind it, and with the profound cultural foundation of Tongji University, TJAD has accumulated a rich experience in both engineering design and technical consultancy, progressing notably over the last sixty-five years. TJAD is a design institution with one of the most extensive design qualifications in China, with a business scope that includes consulting, engineering design, project management, geotechnical engineering, and geological exploration in the fields of building engineering, road engineering, municipal engineering, landscape engineering, environmental pollution prevention, and conservation of historical and cultural relics, among others. The organization has embarked on thousands of projects in China, Africa, and South America that include, among many, Shanghai Tower, Fangfei Garden of the Diaoyutai State Guest House, Table Tennis Gymnasium of the 2008 Olympic Games, African Union Conference Center, New Jinggangshan Revolution Museum, Shanghai Xintiandi, Theme Pavilion of the 2010 Shanghai Expo, Shanghai International Tourist Resort, Shanghai Natural History Museum, Shanghai Symphony Orchestra Concert Hall, China Corporate United Pavilion of Expo 2015 Milan, Havana Hotel of Cuba, Saikang Di Stadium of the Republic of Ghana, the National Arts Center of the Republic of Trinidad and Tobago, Sutong Yangtze River Highway Bridge, and Shanghai A5 (Jiading-Jinshan) Expressway Project.

Shanghai Tower (Cooperative Design, in partnership with Gensler, Cosentini, and Thornton Tomasetti)

Museum of Art Pudong (Cooperative Design, in partnership with Ateliers Jean Nouvel)

Xi'an International Convention and Exhibition Center (Cooperative Design, in partnership with gmp and WES)

TJAD employs more than five thousand outstanding architectural design and engineering personnel to provide top engineering consulting services for our clients, and we have been working hard to promote urban development, so that we may build a better life for citizens through our many professional practices.

We firmly believe that it is the trust that our clients have in us that gives TJAD opportunities to grow. As part of the society and industry, we strive to continue to channel unremitting efforts toward industry development and social progress, just like we have been doing the past sixty-four years.

Contingency and Temporary Medical Building of Shanghai Public Health Clinical Center

Shangyin Opera House (Cooperative Design, in partnership with Christian de Portzamparc, Xu-Acoustique, and Theater Projects Consultants)